25 Projects
for Outdoorsmen

Books by Peter J. Fiduccia

Whitetail Strategies

The Quotable Hunter

North America's Greatest Whitetail Lodges & Outfitters

101 Deer Hunting Tips

Whitetail Strategies, Vol. II

Plant It and They Will Come!

25 Projects
for Outdoorsmen

Quick and Easy Plans
for the Backcountry
and the Backyard

Leo Somma
and
Peter J. Fiduccia

Photographs by Peter J. Fiduccia
Illustrations by Chris Armstrong

The Lyons Press
Guilford, Connecticut
An imprint of The Globe Pequot Press

The Lyons Press is an imprint of The Globe Pequot Press.

10 9 8 7 6 5 4 3 2 1

Printed in the United States

ISBN: 978-1-59228-881-6

Contents

Acknowledgments

for Leo Somma

To my father who gave my twin brother Ralph and I the opportunity to work by his side at twelve years old. He allowed us to use his tools with utmost confidence and pride. We learned by watching him tackle projects in our own home. Our dad instilled the sense of workmanship and pride that comes after completing a project on your own. He gave us the desire to participate in afternoon public-school woodworking shop classes in junior high school, where we made projects ranging from wooden lamps with pull chains to bowls and pieces of furniture to large wooden model sailboats. It was during these classes that we built our first outdoorsman's project, which was a gun cabinet.

To my wife Beth who encouraged me to take on the project of writing this book. I appreciate her confidence in my ability and her willingness in allowing me to spend the extra time at our farm to build many of these projects.

To my cousin Peter whose confidence in me allowed me to coauthor a book in which we have been able to share our passion for the outdoors while building these useful and practical projects to use at our family farm and deer cabin.

To my sons Matthew and Michael and my nephew Cody who worked by my side building the tree stands in this book.

for Peter J. Fiduccia

To my wife Kate for her unwavering support in any undertaking I venture to do. Without her strength, love, and professional skills I would not be where I am today. And to my son Cody who makes me more proud of his many achievements with each passing day. I love you both more than words can describe. And to Leo for all the skills and knowledge you brought to this book without you it could never have been achieved.

Introduction

Like my friends Leo Somma and Peter Fiduccia, I'm a deer hunter. Each November finds me sitting in a permanent tree stand somewhere in New York's Catskill Mountains, watching a game trail, hoping a big whitetail buck will come by.

If you're a deer hunter, sooner or later you're going to climb into a tree to get above the whitetail's uncanny ability to see movement or detect human odor. And unless you want to buy a bunch of expensive, prefab portable tree stands, you're eventually going to build a permanent tree stand in a promising location. I've built a lot of them over the years, too, from simple V-shaped ground blinds consisting entirely of saplings, to more complex tree stands made out of pressure-treated 2x4s and 2x6s, with ladders, railings, and roofs, all held together with 16-penny nails and wood deck screws.

When you're building tree stands, what it all comes down to is being adaptable. Set plans may not work for the situation at hand. Then you have to figure out something that will work, and that requires some ingenuity on your part.

That's what I liked when I read *25 Projects for Outdoorsmen*. Leo and Peter have obviously put a lot of thought into every one of the do-it-yourself projects found in this book. They know how to build things correctly, and it shows on every page. The tool and material list, the cutting schedule for each project, the easy-to-follow diagrams—it's all right there. Follow the instructions and you'll end up with the tree stand, gun rack, or birdhouse that you see in the photo at the beginning of each project.

You can also change any of the designs without great difficulty, and that is what makes this book so useful. Is the Buddy Sidekick stand too big for you? Then you can make it smaller. Don't have a grouping of trees that allows you to add three railings to the Master Hunter's Tree Stand? Then don't; add one or two. The point is, you can take Leo and Peter's basic designs and adapt them to your situation.

The book is not just about tree stands, of course. There are indoor projects, for bookcases, rod holders, and hat racks; and outdoor projects, for bat houses, shooting tables, and garden gates. The firewood storage shed, in particular, is something that I am planning to build as soon as possible. Like Leo, I hate having to clean up all of the wood chips, leaves, twigs, and bugs that end up on my cabin floor whenever I bring in a new batch of wood. Also like Leo, I've looked at wood boxes in some of the local hardware and fireplace stores but found them to be too small for my needs. The box in Chapter 5 will solve my problems. But because the fire box in my wood stove is on the small side, I may make my firewood box just a bit larger, so I can stack two rows of short logs instead of one row of large logs.

Changing plans, altering a design fit your needs, adding your own style—that's half the fun of doing projects like this. *25 Projects for Outdoorsmen* will help you get started.

Jay Cassell
Deputy Editor, Field & Stream *Magazine*
8/21/06

25 Projects
for Outdoorsmen

CHAPTER 1

Safety First

The designs and building methods used for the projects in this book—especially the tree stands—have been reviewed for safety. We cannot overstate the importance of keeping safety uppermost in your mind as you work. When using tools, accidents often happen without warning, allowing little or no time to react. Your reflexes simply aren't fast enough to prevent many injuries, so work smart.

Below are what many might consider the basic dos and don'ts of building, but these rules are worth repeating. While this list is full of helpful reminders, nothing here replaces good old common sense when it comes to safety. Always use the safest construction methods when building any project.

SAFETY REMINDERS

- Never use any tool without first reading the manufacturer's instructions—especially the warnings and cautions. Do not force your tools to do anything they were not designed to do.

- When using power tools, check that circuits aren't overloaded and that all outlets and tools are properly grounded. Refrain from using electric power tools in wet places. Use Ground Fault Circuit Interrup (GFCI) receptacles or extension cords equipped with GFCI protection.

- When undertaking any of the projects in this book, apply caution at every turn: wear ear, hand, and eye protection at all times.

- Wear a disposable face mask when creating dust by sawing or sanding.

- Always keep your hands away from blades, cutters, bits, and saw teeth.

- Never work on projects when you are tired, or when taking medication.

- Work only in well-lighted areas (inside or outside).
- Never work on tree stands without wearing a safety belt. Secure ladders firmly to an anchored support using ratchet straps, and make sure the base of the ladder is level and stable before starting work.
- Never wear loose clothing when using power tools.
- Never work with dull tools.
- Before cutting any piece, be sure it is securely clamped or anchored down to a safe work surface.
- Never stretch to secure a bolt, nail, or screw, or to perform any task. It is always safer to move the ladder or other support than to risk serious injury from a fall.

CHAPTER 2

Tools and Materials

This book walks you through the process of creating indoor and outdoor wooden projects for your lodge, camp, or home. All of these projects are designed to be practical as well as fun to build and use. Each project can be built quickly, and most of the work can be managed on your own. A few projects, however, require an extra set of hands. Do not hesitate to ask for help when you need it. In some cases—like building tree stands—working solo is not only impractical but also unsafe.

TOOLS

As you build the projects in this book, remember the old adage "tools make the job easier." By using the right tools you save yourself time, money, and needless aggravation. Before you spend a single cent on lumber, make sure you purchase the right tools for the job at hand. Quality tools treated with proper care and maintenance can last you a lifetime. They'll also help you build projects that you can be proud of.

Described below are some of the tools needed to make the various projects in this book. In today's market, quality, technically advanced tools are available at affordable prices. You may decide to add to the list or get started with fewer tools; some of the projects in this book require only a few tools.

The tools are broken into three different categories: hand tools, power tools, and bits and blades. Many of these projects can be made using only hand tools, but power tools make the job quicker, easier, and sometimes safer.

Browse through the tools carefully and check out whatever tickles your fancy on the Web sites of the included sources. You can also visit your local hardware store or home center to take a closer look at the tools available. Swing a few hammers while you're there, and look for tools that fit comfortably in both your hands and your budget.

Recommended Hand Tools

TOOL	MODEL NUMBER	SOURCE	DESCRIPTION
Hammer	Craftsman 16 oz. Rip Claw Hammer Model #3821	Sears	Hammers vary in shape, size, length, weight, and material. Use the hammer that fits best in your hand and that you can swing comfortably for long periods of time. Look for a hammer between 16 and 24 ounces. The claw should be used only to remove nails.
Handsaw	Craftsman 20 in. Hand Saw Model #XP2030-500-SEA	Sears	Handsaws come in an endless variety of sizes and shape. For smaller jobs, they're often more convenient to use than a power tool. A taper-ground saw is best for cutting exterior-grade lumber. A combination saw, which we recommend, will both rip and crosscut.
Miter box	Companion Miter Box with Saw Model #36317	Sears	Miter boxes come in a variety of sizes and materials—wood, metal, or plastic. They all do the same thing: help make true cuts at 90 and 45 degrees. Some of our miter boxes are twenty years old and still working well.
Screwdrivers	Craftsman 12 pc. Screwdriver Set, Powerhouse Model #41619	Sears	The types, sizes, and shapes are endless, but a standard combination set should meet most demands.
Chisels	Craftsman 3 pc. Wood Chisel Set Model #36857	Sears	Chisels come in a variety of shapes and sizes. We recommend a set of three or four, ranging in size from $\frac{1}{4}$ inch to 1 inch.
Carpenter square	Companion 8 in. x 12 in. Carpenter Square Model #39654	Sears	Also known as a speed square, this triangular square is used to measure and check 45- and 90-degree angles.

TOOL	MODEL NUMBER	SOURCE	DESCRIPTION
Combination square	Empire 6 in. Pocket Combination Square Model #255N	Sears	This square is used for measuring 45-degree and 90-degree angles. It also can be used as a depth gauge or ruler.
Torpedo level	Craftsman Solid Aluminum Torpedo Level Model #991-10	Sears	This little device comes in handy when you want to make sure that an object is level, either vertically or horizontally.
Ratchet set	Craftsman 12 pc. Socket Wrench Set Model #34745	Sears	The types and sizes of ratchets are endless. We recommend a standard combination set. If you use metric bolts, nuts, and screws, buy a metric set also.
Wrenches	Craftsman 8 pc. Ratcheting Wrench Set Model #42444	Sears	Again, the types and sizes are endless. We recommend a standard combination set and, if you think you'll need it, a metric set.
Staple gun	Arrow Fastener Professional Staple & Nail Gun Model #T50P9N	Sears	A staple gun comes in handy for stapling cloth, thin wood, or wire mesh.
Tin shears	Ridgid 3 pc. Compound Leverage Snip Set Model 79069	Home Depot	Tin shears are used for cutting metal wire mesh or thin sheet metal.
Shovel	Companion Long Handle Round Point Fiberglass Shovel Model #45011	Sears	We all know what shovels are used for: digging. This one will cover it all.
Tape measure	Craftsman 1 in. x 30 ft. Steel Tape Measure Model #39676	Sears	A tape measure is one tool you can't do without. They come in a variety of sizes and lengths. This 30-foot tape will cover all the jobs in this book.

Recommended Hand Tools cont'd

TOOL	MODEL NUMBER	SOURCE	DESCRIPTION
Wood rasp	Craftsman 10 in. Smooth Shoe Rasp Model #31286	Sears	A metal file or rasp is used for smoothing and shaping wood.
Block plane	Footprint Tools Block Plane, 7 x 1⅝ in. Model #4B	Sears	A block plane is used to smooth and straighten the edges of boards. Whenever possible, cut in the direction of the wood grain.
Hand-pruning saw	Craftsman 10 in. Folding Pruning Saw Model #79476968	Sears	With coarser teeth than a handsaw, pruning saws are used to trim tree limbs. The folding handle makes it easy to carry in your pocket.
Pole saw	Craftsman Pump 'N' Cut Ropeless Tree Pruner Model #92366941	Sears	Similar to a pruning saw, except that the blade is attached to a long, extendable pole enabling you to reach up high into the tree limbs.
Nail set	Craftsman 3 pc. Nail Set Model #781	Sears	Nail sets, used to set the head of a finish nail below the surface of the wood, come in a variety of sizes. A combination set covers them all.
Bar clamps	Jorgensen 18 in. Steel Bar Clamp Model #3718-HD	Sears	Bar clamps come in handy when you need to temporarily secure wood or steady a work piece to a table for sawing, drilling, or sanding.

Recommended Power Tools

TOOL	MODEL NUMBER	SOURCE	DESCRIPTION
Table saw	Skil 10 in. Table Saw Model #3400-08	Sears	Used to make straight or angled cuts, table saws are much more accurate than circular saws and come in a variety of sizes. We recommend a 10-inch model.
	Craftsman 10 in. Table Saw Model #OR35505	Sears	
	Bosch 10 in. Worksite Table Saw with Folding Stand Model #4000-07	Home Depot	
Cordless drill	Skil 14.4 Volt Cordless Drill/Driver with Built-in Bit Size Indicator Model #2567-02	Sears	A cordless drill is a handy in any shop and a must-have in the field. Available in a variety of sizes, they are used to drill holes, of course. When outfitted with a driver bit, you can also drive screws with them.
	Craftsman 14.4 Volt Cordless Drill/Driver with Laser Model #11540	Sears	
	Bosch 14.4V Brute Tough ½ in. Cordless Drill Driver Model #33614-2G	Home Depot	
Power drill	Skil ½ in. Drill Model #6325-11	Sears	Similar to the cordless drill except it can only be used where you have access to power. The advantage of this over the cordless drill is that you don't have to worry about the battery depleting.
	Bosch ½ in. High-Speed Drill Model 1013VSR	Home Depot	
Router	Skil 2HP Fixed-base Router w/Built-In Worklight Model #1815	Sears	Used with a variety of bits to profile or mill the edges and faces of wood.
	Bosch 2 HP Fixed-Base Router Model #1617	Home Depot	

Recommended Power Tools cont'd

TOOL	MODEL NUMBER	SOURCE	DESCRIPTION
Random-orbit sander	Bosch 5 in. Random Orbit Palm Sander/Polisher Model 1295D	Home Depot	A hand-held electric sander that both orbits and spins to smooth surfaces.
Belt sander	Skil 3 in. x 18 in. Belt Sander Model #7500	Sears	A handheld electric sander used to make sanding large surfaces much easier. As opposed to random-orbit sanders, belt sanders are for the bigger projects. Take care to avoid "digging" into the wood with aggressive grits.
	Bosch 3 in. x 21 in. Variable Speed Belt Sander Model #1274DVS	Home Depot	
Jigsaw	Skil 4680 VS Orbital Scrolling Jigsaw Model #4680-04	Sears	This saw is excellent for making curved, straight, or angled cuts. It is used to cut out holes for windows, doors, or round shapes. A variety of blades can be used depending on what you're cutting. Both powered and cordless models are available.
	Bosch 24V Cordless Jigsaw Kit Model #52324	Home Depot	
Screw gun	Skil iXO Cordless Palm Size Screwdriver #2336	Sears	A screw gun is used solely for driving and removing screws. It'll drive screws with a fraction of the work and time spent wrestling an old-fashioned screwdriver.
	Craftsman Companion 4.8 Volt Pistol Screwdriver Model #10175	Sears	
	Bosch 12V Compact Tough Cordless Drill/Driver Model #32612	Home Depot	
Chain saw	Craftsman 18 in. Gas Chain Saw Model #358350820	Sears	Chain saws come in various sizes specified by the chain length. Don't bother with electric powered chain saws—go for the more versatile gas-powered saw. The 18-inch model will cover most jobs.

TOOL	MODEL NUMBER	SOURCE	DESCRIPTION
Air-powered nail gun	Paslode 16-gauge Cordless Straight Finish Nailer Model #902000	Home Depot	Nail guns come in a variety of sizes and brands, with the air power provided by either air compressors or cartridges for the portable versions. We suggest buying the portable model, as it's particularly handy in the field. A variety of nail sizes can be used depending on the type of gun.
Compound miter saw	Craftsman 12 in. Compound Miter Saw Model #9-21215	Sears	This stationary saw is used to make straight or angled cuts. The wood is placed on the bottom table, and the blade is brought down on the wood to make the cut. Once you use one to make a miter cut, you will never want to use a hand miter box again.
	Makita LS1013 10 in. Slide Dual Compound Miter Saw Model #LS1013	Home Depot	
	Bosch 10 in. Slide Compound Miter Saw Model #3915	Home Depot	
Radial arm saw	Craftsman Professional Laser Trac 10 inch Radial Arm Saw Model #22010	Sears	Stationary electric saws used to cut wood straight or can be used to make angle cuts. They come in a variety of sizes, but a 10-inch saw will cover most of your needs. This saw differs from the table saw in that the blade rides on a guide and is pulled across to make crosscuts. If used for ripping, the blade guide is rotated 90 degrees and then the wood is pushed toward the blade as with a table saw, except that the blade cuts from the top as opposed to the bottom on a table saw.
	Delta 33–895X 12 inch Radial Arm Saw		

Recommended Bits and Blades

TOOL	MODEL NUMBER	SOURCE	DESCRIPTION
Drill bit set	Milwaukee 29 Piece Jobbers Twist Drill Bit Kit Model #48-89-0010	Sears	The most common type of drill bit is the twist drill bit, which can be used to drill holes in wood or metal. Since the drill bits vary in size, we suggest purchasing a combination kit.

Recommended Bits and Blades cont'd

TOOL	MODEL NUMBER	SOURCE	DESCRIPTION
Router bit set	Skil 24 Piece Carbide Router Bit Set in Wooden Storage Case Model #91024 24	Sears	Router bits come in a wide variety of sizes and cutting profiles. The ¼-inch shank is the most popular. Again, a combination kit is a good choice.
Hole saw set	Bosch Power Change Bi-Metal Hole Saw Master Set (11 pc) Model #PC11PCM	Home Depot	Hole saws are used with a drill to cut holes in wood. They vary in size from ⅜-inch up to 5-inch. A combination set provides most of the sizes needed in this book.

MATERIALS

The materials used in this book include various wood species, fasteners, and finishing products. Each project lists the sizes and types of wood required, as well as the types of fasteners we suggest. The finishing products are those we recommend, but can be altered according to your tastes.

The type of lumber you use depends on whether the project is intended for outdoor or indoor use. If the project will be exposed to weather, choose a wood that is durable, long-lasting, and resistant to moisture and insects. If the project is intended for indoor use, feel free to use whatever species of wood suits your tastes. The woods we suggest are those we used to build the actual projects pictured in this book.

The exterior wood most commonly used for these projects is exterior-grade lumber, such as ACQ (alkaline copper quaternary) or cedar. ACQ-treated lumber is treated with a preservative that contains copper and quaternary ammonium compound (quat), as opposed to the earlier CCA lumber, which contained arsenic. ACQ lumber is now the wood of choice for outdoor construction. Cedar is fairly lightweight and is very easy to work with. Other exterior woods like redwood and mahogany are also available, but they usually cost more. We chose the more affordable lumber for most of the projects seen here.

Pine, Douglas fir, oak, and poplar are all common choices for interior projects. Pine is relatively inexpensive and easy to work with, and it finishes nicely with either stain or a clear finish. Douglas fir is often used for interior framing and is also easy to work with. If you're aiming for a richer-looking project, consider using a hardwood like oak. Oak is more expensive and a bit more difficult to cut, but it finishes nicely with either a clear finish or a stain. For projects that will be painted, poplar is often my wood of choice. Poplar is harder than pine or fir, but much easier to work than oak. It also looks great with a painted finish.

For each of the projects, we provide a materials list that covers all of the lumber needed. We list the actual size of the lumber, as opposed to the nominal dimension of standard lumber. For example, a nominal 1x6 board actually measures $3/4$ x $5^1/_2$ inches, a 2x4 measures $1^1/_2$ inch x $3^1/_2$ inches, a 2x10 measures $1^1/_2$ inches x $9^1/_4$ inches, and so on. Keep this discrepancy in mind as you shop for lumber.

Nails and screws make up the bulk of the fasteners used in these projects. For interior use, nails and screws do not have to be corrosion-resistant—look for common or bright nails and uncoated screws. For exterior use, nails and screws should be made of brass or stainless steel, or covered with a protective coating. Because brass and stainless-steel screws tend to be more expensive, we used coated fasteners. The most common coated fasteners are galvanized, anodized, or zinc-plated. Galvanized nails and screws are also the least expensive, but should not be used with ACQ lumber—the alkaline copper quaternary coating will cause the nails to corrode. There are a variety of fasteners designed for use with ACQ, so check with your supplier to make sure you get the proper type.

Your choice of finish depends on where your project will be placed and how it will blend with your existing décor. Some of the woods, such as cedar and oak, look good with only a clear finish like varnish, polyurethane, or shellac. They can also be stained to your desired color or shade, left unfinished, or coated with a clear finish after staining. If you choose to paint any of these projects, we recommend a latex-based paint. When painting an outdoor project, be sure to use an exterior-grade paint, stain, or clear finish.

CHAPTER 3

Projects for the Hunter and Outdoorsman

- Two-Gun Deer-Hoof Wall Rack
- Freestanding Nine-Gun Rack
- Ammo Box
- Fishing Rod Holder
- Hunter's Hat Rack
- Wall Plaque for Mounted Game

Two-Gun Deer-Hoof Wall Rack

Back in the early seventies, we used the basement of my home in Warwick, New York, as our deer camp. During those days the area was rural, and most of our deer hunting took place on the farms and mountains that surrounded the house.

In order not to track dirt into the upper level, we finished off the basement into a large area where we could leave our muddy boots, wet clothes, hunting gear, and, of course, our firearms. Each hunter had his or her own area, and all of his or her equipment was neatly stored there.

As time went on, we upgraded our "deer camp at home" to include several wooden projects that helped to organize the area. One of the first projects was the Two-Gun Deer-Hoof Wall Rack. It hung on the wall in the entrance to the garage. As soon as one of the hunters returned to our "camp" for morning coffee or lunch, or at the end of the day's hunt, he or she could unload outside, walk in, and hang his or her firearm on one of the four gun racks there.

The style of this rack provides easy placement of rifles on the deer hooves. The barrel rests securely on one hoof and the stock firmly on the other. Removing the firearm from the rack is just as convenient.

Modifying this project doesn't take much either. If the need arises in your deer camp, you can make the two-gun rack into a four-gun or even a six-gun rack by simply adding width to the backboard where the deer hooves are attached.

So the next time you take a buck or doe, remember to remove the hoof from the leg at the second joint. One deer, obviously, will provide enough hooves to make your first two-gun rack. A taxidermist must prepare the hooves, and the cost is very affordable.

This unit is not only very functional, but also provides any deer camp, trophy room, or home with a unique gun mount that lends a "deer" theme to the area. It tells everyone you're not only a deer hunter, but one who utilizes every part of the deer you bag.

This is a terrific project to get started on because it is both simple to build and useful. For obvious safety reasons, if you decide to keep your guns hanging in an open room, especially where children can reach them, we strongly recommend that you store them with trigger locks in place. We made this rack using knotty pine, but you can use any other wood and finish it as you desire.

Two-Gun Deer-Hoof Wall Rack

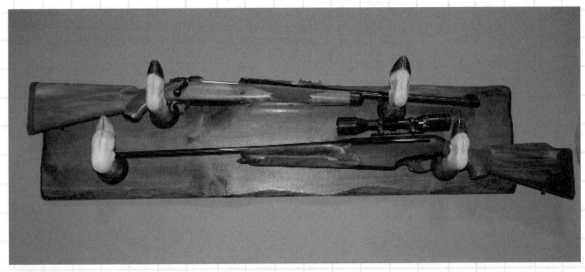

Overall Size: 11½ in. wide, 48 in. long

Tools Needed

- Handsaw or table saw
- Router with ½-inch round-over bit
- Wood file
- Drill
- Drill bit, ¼-inch
- Hole saw, ½-inch
- Socket wrench
- Hand sander or sandpaper
- Level

Materials

- Four ¼ x 20-inch nuts and washers
- Two ½-inch ring hangers with mounting screws
- Green felt, 12 inches by 48 inches
- White glue
- Stain
- Finishing material such as varnish or shellac
- Two wood screws or heavy-duty picture hangers

Cutting List

	Part	Dimensions	Qty.	Material
A	Wall board	1½ in. x 11½ in. x 48 in.	1	Knotty pine
B	Gun holders	~ 4 in. x 4 in.	4	Deer hooves

Note: Measurements reflect the actual thickness of dimension lumber.

Building the Two-Gun Deer-Hoof Wall Rack

Prepare the wall board

1. Using a table saw or circular saw, cut the wall board (A) to size as shown in the drawing.

2. Finish off the front edge of the wall board using a router outfitted with a ½-inch round-over bit. If a router is not available, use a wood file to round off the edges.

3. Roughen the edges with a wood file. You can shape the edges in a pattern similar to the one shown in the photo or in any pattern you prefer.

4. Drill ¼-inch holes through the wallboard, locating them as shown in the drawing.

5. In these same holes, drill ½-inch-diameter recesses approximately ½ inch deep. Begin

Two-Gun Deer-Hoof Wall Rack cont'd

FIGURE 1

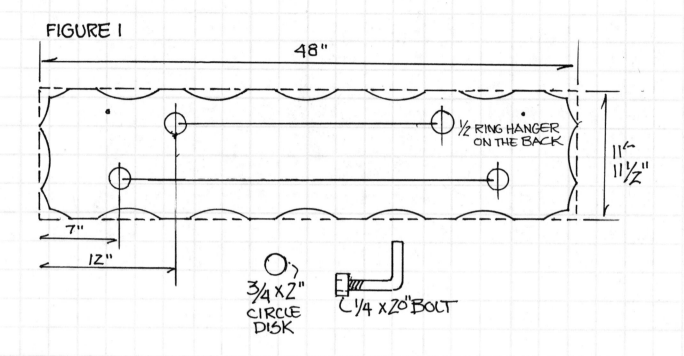

drilling from the back of the wall board and take care to stop before you break through the front.

Mount the deer hooves

1. Use hooves that a taxidermist has prepared. Make sure he finishes the backs of the hooves with ¼ x 20-inch threaded bolts. The ends of the bolts should extend ¾ inch from the backs of hooves.
2. Mount the hooves to the wall rack using ¼-inch flat washers and nuts. Tighten the nuts using a socket wrench.
3. Cut a piece of green felt in the same shape as the wall board. Use regular white glue to attach the felt to the back of the wall board.
4. Mount two ring hangers on the back of the wall board. They should be placed 2 inches from the top and approximately 6 inches from each edge.

Apply the finishing touches

1. Finish-sand the board, either by hand or machine.
2. Apply a coat of stain in the color of your choice. Then lay on two coats of shellac or varnish, allowing it to dry fully between coats.

Mount the wall rack

1. You can mount the shelf anywhere on a wall using wood screws or heavy-duty picture hangers. Line up the back hanger holes and mark out the locations. Use a level when locating the anchors or screws on the wall. If there are no studs in the area, use anchors to secure the screws.

Freestanding Nine-Gun Rack

As the morning hunt came to an end, we all met back at the house to warm up, have some breakfast, and plan a small push through our swamp. Once on the deck, we all instinctively checked our firearms to make sure they were unloaded and then hung them from hooks we had on the deck.

While some of us were busy cooking breakfast and others showered or cat-napped, we were unaware of how hard the wind had begun to blow. In fact, it had kicked up to 30 miles per hour. Yup, you guessed it, hard enough to blow a few guns off their hooks, which were screwed in very sturdily.

As we sat down to eat breakfast, we all heard a heavy "thump" sound coming from the deck. It didn't take any of us long to realize a rifle had fallen from its perch. Several of us dashed outside, and to our horror and surprise, there were three firearms lying on the deck with the wind trying its best to dislodge the others.

Needless to say, the guys who owned the fallen firearms were really pissed off (excuse my French). Now they had to run up to the range and make sure their guns were still zeroed in. We decided right then and there that we needed a safe indoor place to shelve our firearms as soon as possible. Once again, Leo and his woodworking skills came to the rescue.

This is the gun rack he made from edge-glued and screwed pine boards. It makes a nice addition to any hunting camp, cabin, trophy room, den, or home (if children are at home, be sure trigger locks are installed on all the guns).

Over time, we've learned how convenient it is when everyone comes back from a hunt and has an orderly place to store their firearms. This rack can be made to hold any number of guns. The design includes instructions for making a nine-gun rack, but you can adjust the size if you want the rack to hold more or fewer firearms. The finished rack can be stained, varnished, painted, or waxed, depending on your tastes.

Freestanding Nine-Gun Rack

Tools Needed

- Table saw or circular saw
- Block plane
- Jigsaw
- Belt sander, random-orbit sander, or sandpaper
- Hole saw
- Backsaw or table saw
- Drill
- $\frac{1}{2}$ inch chisel

Materials

- Oak-tag or brown paper
- Wood glue
- Wood screws, $1\frac{3}{4}$-inch
- Mushroom-style button plugs
- Finishing material, such as stain, lacquer, or varnish

Overall Size: 36 in. long, 43 in. high, 12 in. deep

Cutting List

	Part	Dimensions	Qty.	Material
A	Top back	1 in. x $4\frac{1}{2}$ in. x $33\frac{1}{2}$ in.	1	5/4 pine
B	Top gun holder	1 in. x 6 in. x $33\frac{1}{2}$ in.	1	5/4 pine
C	Sides	1 in. x 12 in. x 43 in.	2	5/4 pine
D	Bottom	1 in. x $11\frac{1}{8}$ in. x $11\frac{3}{8}$ in.	1	5/4 pine
E	Lower butt holder	1 in. x 9 in. x $33\frac{1}{2}$ in.	1	5/4 pine
F	Bottom corners	1 in. x $4\frac{3}{4}$ in. x $9\frac{1}{2}$ in.	2	5/4 pine

Note: Measurements reflect the actual thickness of dimension lumber.

Building the Freestanding Nine-Gun Rack

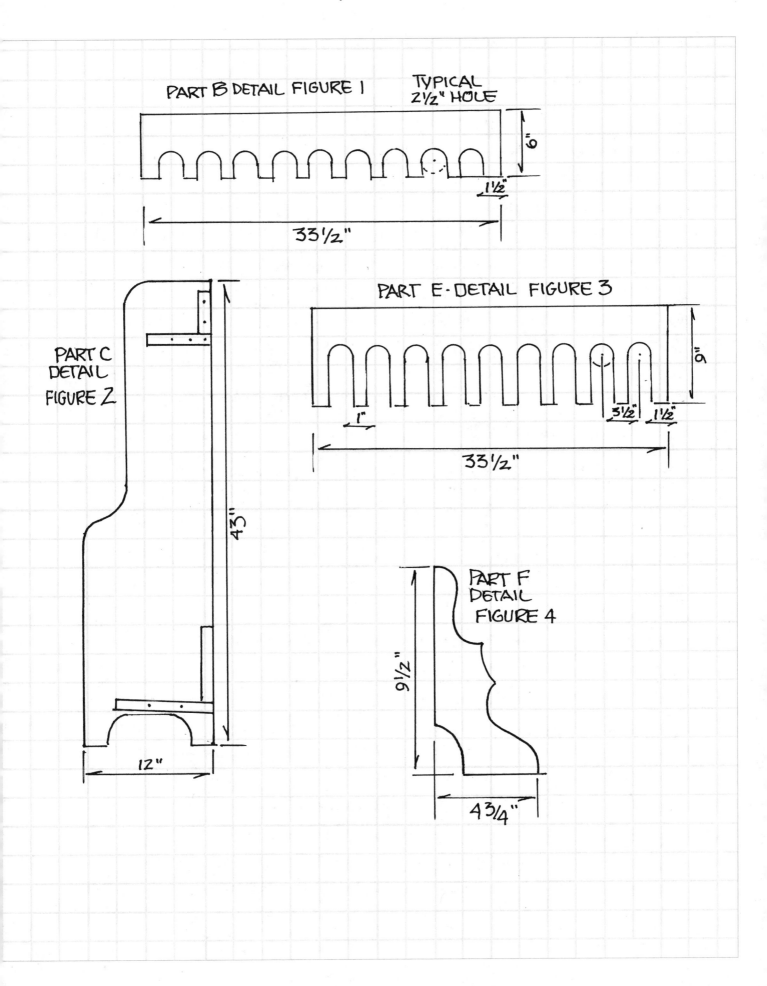

PART B DETAIL FIGURE 1   TYPICAL 2½" HOLE

6"

1½"

33½"

PART C
DETAIL
FIGURE 2

43"

12"

PART E·DETAIL FIGURE 3

9"

1"   3½"   1½"

33½"

PART F
DETAIL
FIGURE 4

9½"

4¾"

Freestanding Nine-Gun Rack cont'd

Make the sides, top back, bottom, and bottom corners

1. Use a table saw or circular saw to cut the sides (C) to length and width from $5/4$ stock that is 14 inches wide. If you make the cuts with a circular saw, use a block plane to smooth and square any rough edges.
2. Mark out the shape of both sides using the pattern provided in the drawing. Then cut out the shape using a jigsaw. Sand the curved edges smooth with a drum sander, belt sander, or by hand. Repeat for the other side, and make the cutout.
3. Cut the top back (A) to length from $5/4$ x 5-inch pine stock.
4. Cut the bottom (D) to length from $5/4$ x 12-inch stock.
5. Transfer the bottom corner patterns (F) to two pieces of $5/4$ x 5 x 10-inch pine. Cut to the line using a jigsaw and sand the edges smooth. Using the patterns shown in figures 1, 2, 3, and 4, draw the actual shapes on pieces of oak-tag or brown paper based on the scaled dimensions. Trace the patterns onto the appropriate pieces of wood, as stated above.

Make the top gun and lower butt holders

1. Make the top gun holder (B) and lower butt holder (E) to length and width.
2. Measure and mark the center points for the nine butt-holder holes (see figure 3). Drill the holes using a $2\frac{1}{2}$-inch hole saw.
3. Complete the butt-holder cutouts using a backsaw or table saw to ensure straight cuts into the edges of the holes.
4. Repeat step 2 for each of the nine slots in the top gun holder (see figure 1).
5. Sand all the rough edges before assembly.

Mount the top gun holder and lower butt holder

1. Drill five $1/16$-inch pilot holes in the bottom portion of the top gun holder (B), approximately $1/2$ inch in from the straight edge.
2. Screw through these holes to mount the top back (A) along the edge. For insurance, reinforce the screwed joint with wood glue.
3. Place the lower butt holder (E) on top of the bottom (D), so that the front opening of the butt holder is 2 inches from the front edge of the bottom (D). Use glue and wood screws from the underside of the bottom to secure the lower butt holder in place.

Assemble the upper and lower assemblies

1. Drill $1/16$-inch pilot holes through the outside of both sides (C) at the locations shown in the drawing.
2. Drill $3/8$-inch counter-bored holes approximately $1/4$ inch deep into the same locations. These recesses allow you to set the screw heads below the surface of the wood.
3. Mount both the upper and lower assemblies using $1\frac{3}{4}$-inch wood screws and wood glue.
4. Mount the bottom corners (F) in place using glue and wood screws.

Apply the finishing touches

1. Scrape off any excess glue using a $1/2$-inch chisel or damp cloth.
2. Sand all the edges and faces smooth.
3. To hide the screw heads, apply a small amount of glue onto mushroom-style wooden plugs. Then tap the plugs into place in all the counter-bored holes.
4. Apply your desired finish, allowing for drying time between coats.

Ammo Box

If there is one project in this book that we both consider a must-have for camp or home, it's the Ammo Box. It makes the storage of ammo convenient and safe. If you have a deer camp that is a bit crowded and space is at a premium, then this handy little item becomes even more valuable.

Years ago I hunted at a deer camp in Hancock, New York, called the Ridge Runners, a name garnered from the steep ridges and mountainsides that encompassed the 2,000 acres of property. There were a lot of hunters in this camp, and we all slept in one very large room where single beds and cots lined all four walls. Each bed had a small nightstand that had a light and two drawers. There were several clothing hooks to hang your hunting gear on above each bed. By now I'm sure you're getting the picture: private space was at a premium and everyone was quite protective of his or her real estate.

I stored as much as I could in the two drawers, but that mostly included things like my wallet, watch, and knife. I used the space under my bed to store larger items like my boots, bow and rifle cases, and, most importantly, my ammo box. Each morning when I grabbed my rifle, I simply opened the box, took out my shells, and slid the box back under the bed. If your deer camp is a bit crowded—like the one I just described—having a safe and convenient place to store your ammo can help tremendously.

We both think that it is also important to have several different-size boxes to segregate different-size shells and bullets. Not only does it make it easier to find what you're looking for, it also helps to ensure that you have grabbed the right size ammo as well. For example, I regularly shoot both a .270 and .280 caliber for thin-skinned big game. Keeping the two types of ammo apart from each other by storing them in separate ammo boxes is both helpful and safe.

The ammo box shown here is large enough to hold up to twenty-four boxes of shotgun shells—about 600 shells. The boxes are stored with twelve on the bottom and another twelve resting on top. The box can be made larger, but remember that the bigger it is, the heavier it is to lug around.

Obviously, the ammo box can be made smaller as well, which may be a good idea if you plan to store only bullets. Although not shown here, it's easy to modify this design so that it includes a removable lift-out tray. The tray would be approximately 1½ inches in height, divided into two or three separate bays, and placed so that it sits flush with the top of the box when the cover is removed. Trays are good for conveniently holding some of the smaller accessories you need—cleaners, separate shells, patches, and so on.

For the box pictured here, we used pine to keep the expenses down, but cedar, poplar, or a hardwood such as oak could be used instead. The box can be left unfinished; rubbed with linseed oil, shellac, or varnish; or stained or painted to suit your tastes.

Ammo Box

Tools Needed

- Table saw or handsaw
- Block plane
- Hammer
- Chisel or router with a ¾-inch coving bit
- Nail set

Materials

- Wood glue
- 4d and 6d finish nails
- One 18-inch-long piano hinge, ½ inch wide, with screws
- Wood putty
- Sandpaper
- Finishing materials such as stain, shellac, varnish, linseed oil, or paint

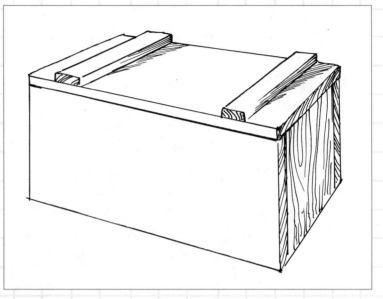

Overall Size: 18 in. long, 11 in. deep, 11½ in. high

Cutting List

	Part	Dimensions	Qty.	Material
A	Top cover	¾ in. x 18 in. x 11 in.	1	Pine
B	Front and back	¾ in. x 18 in. x 10¾ in.	2	Pine
C	Sides	¾ in. x 9½ in. x 10¾ in.	2	Pine
D	Bottom	¾ in. x 16½ in. x 9½ in.	1	Pine
E	Top stretchers	¾ in. x 1½ in. x 11 in.	2	Pine

Note: Measurements reflect the actual thickness of dimension lumber.

Building the Ammo Box

Cut the parts and build the box

1. Cut all the pieces (A, B, C, D, and E) to the desired lengths and widths using a table saw or handsaw. If you use a handsaw, smooth and square all the edges with a block plane.
2. Lay out the bottom (D) on a flat work surface.
3. Place one of the sides (C) against the side edge of the bottom (D). Use wood glue and 6d finish nails to secure it in place. Repeat this process to attach the other side to the bottom of the box.

4. Place the front (B) against the front edge of the bottom (D), making sure that the ends are flush with each of the sides. Use wood glue and 6d finish nails to attach it to both the bottom edge and the sides. We used five nails at the bottom and four to secure each side. Repeat the process to attach the back.

Assemble the top cover

1. To mortise for the hinge, cut a ¹⁄₁₆-inch deep groove ¾ inch wide and 18 inches long on the

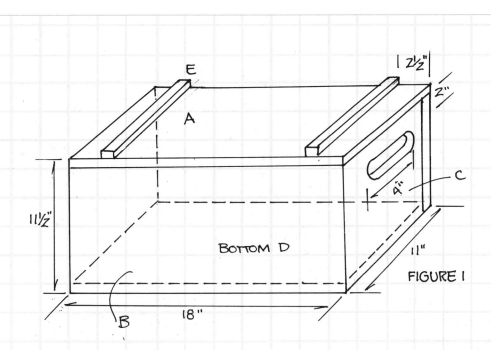

E

A

2½"

2"

11½"

C

4"

BOTTOM D

11"

FIGURE 1

B   18"

top edge of the back and another on the underside of the back edge of the top cover (A). This mortise cut can be made using a chisel or with a router outfitted with a straight bit set to a depth of $1/16$ inch.

2. Using the small wood screws provided with the hinge, attach the piano hinge to the top cover and then the top of the back.

3. Place the two top stretchers (E) on the top cover, approximately 2 inches in from each edge. Use wood glue and 4d finish nails to secure the stretchers (E) in place.

Apply the finishing touches

1. Cut out the side handles after the box has been assembled. Use a router with a ¾-inch round-nose bit to carefully rout recesses as shown in figure 1. You will need to make a guide to obtain a straight cut. Make the cut approximately 4 inches long, and $3/8$ inch deep on each side. If a router is not available, this cut can be made using a hand round face chisel.

2. Set all nail heads using the nail set and then fill all the visible holes with wood putty.

3. Sand the edges and surfaces to whatever smoothness you desire.

4. We decided not to finish this project, but you can oil it with linseed oil, paint it, stain it, or varnish it as you see fit.

Fishing Rod Holder

I have a pet peeve about storing my fishing rods. If they're not in a secure rod holder, I get very nervous about their safety. I have had too many of my favorite rods broken because they were laid or placed in a spot that made them vulnerable to damage.

I have a large collection of fly rods that includes some very old Fenwick rods (remember their slogan, "I'm a Fenwick man"?), and some more modern rods including Sage, G-Loomis, Orvis, and even a custom-made Chattahoochee bamboo fly rod. I also do a lot of small creek and stream fishing and have a dozen 4-foot-6-inch, 5-foot, and 5-foot-6-inch ultralight rods and spinning reels as well. All of these are stored carefully on my rod racks.

Not only does the rack provide a safe storage area for your rods, but it also adds ambiance to any room—a trophy room, den, library, or game room. It also announces to guests that you are an avid angler who loves to fish and knows how to properly store rods.

I take great pride in my rod racks because they hold the equipment from which I get a great deal of enjoyment and memories. I can vividly remember placing my son Cody's first brand-name rod in one of my racks. It made Kate and I feel so proud that he enjoys fishing as much as we do. It also made us feel good to see him understand the importance of taking care of his equipment (at the time Cody was twelve years old).

I enjoy showing off Leo's talent as well. Everyone who sees this unit remarks about how nice it is. I tell them that it is not only a handsome rod holder, but also a good-looking piece of furniture.

The rod rack is made from oak that has been edge-glued together. It holds rods in an upright position, and the spacing is wide enough that you can store rods with the reels attached. It eliminates storing your rods in cases, on hooks in the garage, or, worse yet, lying flat in the rafters of the basement, barn, or attic. After building this unit you can store up to twelve of your most cherished rods vertically, safely, and within easy reach.

This basic design can be altered to hold any number of rods. We've included instructions for making a twelve-rod rack. To give this piece a furniture-type finish, you can stain it to your choice of color, varnish it, and wax it.

Fishing Rod Holder

Tools Needed

- Table saw
- Drill with $\frac{1}{16}$-inch and $\frac{3}{8}$-inch bit and $1\frac{1}{2}$-inch wood bit or hole saw
- Jigsaw
- Random-orbit sander, belt sander, or sandpaper
- Screw gun or driver bit for your drill
- $\frac{3}{8}$-inch bit
- Four clamps with 24-inch capacity
- $\frac{1}{2}$-inch chisel

Materials

- Oak-tag or brown paper
- Wood glue
- $1\frac{1}{2}$-inch wood screws
- Twelve rubber rod holder clips
- Four $\frac{3}{4}$-inch metal L-brackets
- Mushroom-style button plugs
- Finishing materials

Authors Note: Finding the rubber rod holder clips can be difficult. They are not available everywhere. I located them by doing an Internet search on Google.

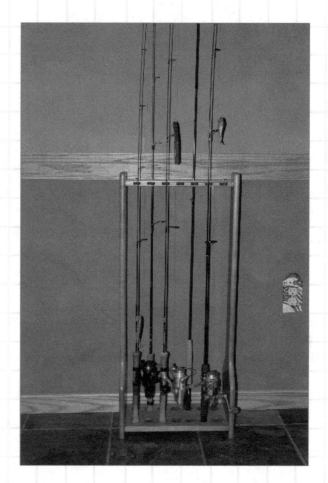

Overall Size: 36 in. high, 11$\frac{1}{2}$ in. deep, 21$\frac{1}{2}$ in. wide

Cutting List

	Part	Dimensions	Qty.	Material
A	Sides	$\frac{3}{4}$ in. x 11$\frac{1}{2}$ in. x 36 in.	2	Oak
B	Bottom rod rest	$\frac{3}{4}$ in. x 10 in. x 19 in.	1	Oak
C	Top rod support	$\frac{3}{4}$ in. x 3$\frac{1}{2}$ in. x 19 in.	1	Oak

Note: Measurements reflect the actual thickness of dimension lumber.

Building the Fishing Rod Holder

Make the sides

1. Cut the sides (A) to length and width using a table saw.
2. Using the pattern for the sides (A) shown in figure 1, draw out the shape on a piece of oak-tag or brown paper and transfer the pattern onto each of the sides (A).
3. Cut the sides (A) to shape using a jigsaw and then smooth the cut with a random-orbit sander, belt sander, or by hand.
4. Pre-drill $\frac{1}{16}$-inch holes in both side pieces at locations as shown in figure 1.
5. Drill $\frac{3}{8}$-inch counter-bored holes approximately $\frac{1}{4}$ inch deep into the $\frac{1}{16}$-inch holes you just drilled. These counter-bored holes will allow the screw heads to rest below the face of the sides (A).

Fishing Rod Holder cont'd

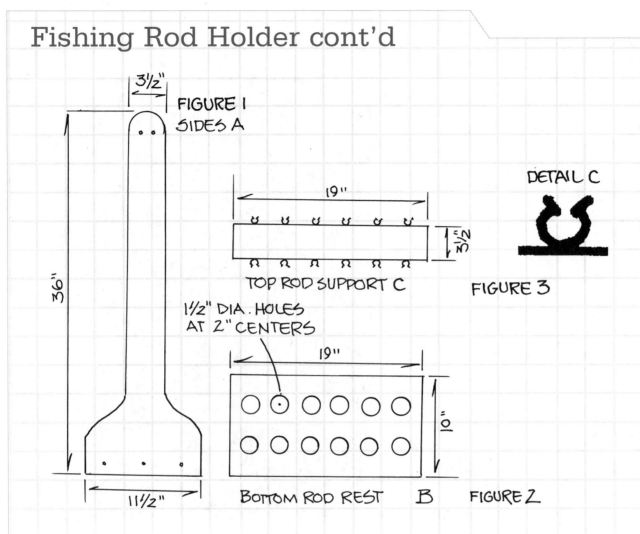

FIGURE 1
SIDES A

3½"

36"

11½"

DETAIL C

FIGURE 3

19"

3½"

TOP ROD SUPPORT C

1½" DIA. HOLES
AT 2" CENTERS

19"

10"

BOTTOM ROD REST   B   FIGURE 2

Make the top rod support and bottom rod rest

1. Cut the top rod support (C) and bottom rod rest (B) to finished length and width at the table saw.
2. Measure and mark center points for the twelve rod holes in the bottom rod rest (B), in figure 2. Drill the holes ¼ inch deep using a 1½-inch-diameter drill bit or hole saw.
3. Measure and mark the location for the six rod holder clips (refer to figure 3) on the front edge of the top rod support (C). Repeat the same process on the opposite side of the top rod support (C).
4. Secure the rod holder clips in place using a screw gun or with a screwdriver bit chucked into your drill.

Attach the top and bottom to the sides

1. Apply glue and use the four clamps to secure the sides to the bottom and top. Both the bot-

tom and top pieces should be inset 1 inch from the top and bottom ends of the side pieces. Drive 1½-inch wood screws through the sides to attach the top and bottom permanently.

2. To add additional support, mount four ¾-inch metal L-brackets on the underside of the bottom rod rest and secure them with wood screws.

Apply the finishing touches.

1. Scrape off any excess glue using a ½-inch chisel or damp cloth.
2. Sand all the faces and edges smooth, either by machine or by hand.
3. Install mushroom-style button plugs in all counter-bored holes using a small amount of glue and a few taps with a block of wood.
4. Apply the finish of your choice.

Hunter's Hat Rack

If you are like me, you're always looking for a place to hang your hunting hat when you come in from the field. No matter how many times I place my hat on a chair, countertop, or gun safe it is *never* there when I want it. It's like putting socks into a dryer: They have a mind of their own and one always decides it is time to escape, leaving only one sock to be found when you need it. Well, hats have the same game plan; they make a break for it every time you lay them down.

Last year, after returning from a hunt to the lodge, I placed my special "lucky" C.C. Filson cap, the one I've worn for years, on my bed during lunch. When I went to retrieve it, it was nowhere to be found. There were only five of us hunting, and no one had gone into my bedroom while we were eating lunch. Nevertheless, the hat was gone. I searched for twenty minutes and then gave up and went out hunting without it. Needless to say, without my lucky hat on, I didn't see a single deer.

When I got back to the house, I looked for it again, to no avail. Later that night I saw some material on the floor. After picking it up I realized it was part of the brim of my Filson hat! I knew what had happened immediately. Our new yellow lab pup, Kira, was the culprit. She must have found the hat on the bed and thought it was a great toy to shred into pieces. Lucky for her she is so cute—otherwise, I'd have scolded her severely for destroying my lucky cap. When I went to confront her, I just couldn't get past that goofy look she gives when she knows she did something I don't approve of.

I went to Leo with hat in hand (or at least parts of hat in hand) and pleaded my case for him to come up with something that we could hang our hats on safely. This project is what he came up with. It has solved the case of the escaping hat and has also prevented any more hats from being chewed up by Kira.

We have since hung two on the deck and two more in the entryway of our hunting camp. Whenever we come in, we place our hats conveniently on the pegs, ready to be picked up when we leave. No more hassle looking for misplaced headgear. I love it.

An added benefit is that the hat rack also helps to quickly dry out a cap that is wet or damp. I hang my hat on the outdoor rack in the evening, which helps to air out any accumulated scent as well.

This is one of those projects: after you make it, you'll wonder how you lived without it. From what I saw while Leo was building it, it was easy to make too. So hats off to you—give this project a try and you will be glad you did!

Hunter's Hat Rack

Overall Size: 24 in. long, 3½ in. wide

Tools Needed

- Table saw or handsaw
- Router and ½-inch round-over bit
- ⅛-inch drill bit
- Drill and ⅛-inch drill bit
- Level

Materials

- Wood glue
- Four #8 wood screws, ¾ inch long
- Two #8 round-head brass wood screws, 2½ inches long
- Sandpaper
- Finishing materials such as stain and varnish

Cutting List

	Part	Dimensions	Qty.	Material
A	Wall back	¾ in. x 3½ in. x 24 in.	1	Knotty pine
B	Clothing pegs	½ in. x 4 in.	4	Pine

Note: Measurements reflect the actual thickness of dimension lumber.

Building the Hunter's Hat Rack

Cut and shape the wall back

1. Cut the wall back (A) to final size using a table saw or handsaw, as shown in figure 1.

2. Shape the top and bottom edges of the front using a router outfitted with a ½-inch round-over bit.

3. On the front of the wall back (A) drill four ⅜-inch holes approximately ½ inch deep and spaced according to the drawing.

4. Drill ⅛-inch mounting holes through to the back of the wall back (A). To make mounting the rack easy, set these holes 16 inches

CHAPTER 4

Country Camp and Home Furnishing

- Hunter's Dressing & Boot Bench
- Basic Bookcase
- Outdoorsman's Picture Frame

Hunter's Dressing & Boot Bench

How many times have you been at deer camp without a comfortable place to put on your boots in the morning? I'll bet it's a lot! If there is one thing that has always annoyed me at deer camps I have been in, it is the lack of places to sit while you're getting ready in the morning. I really dislike standing on one foot and bouncing around while trying to keep my balance as I pull my boot over each foot. We've all been there, eh?

The one project that I insisted on including in this book was a place to put on your boots. Leo gave me this project just to stop me from whining about it. The Hunter's Dressing & Boot Bench is a must-have item for any deer camp, lodge, or even summer home. It makes short work of putting on boots or other shoes comfortably. A highly functional unit, it will seat three adults at one time.

If you add a few upholstered cushions, it becomes not only more comfortable but more stylish as well. And who doesn't want their deer-camp furniture to look stylish? My wife hunts as well, so keeping our projects from looking like they belong in a manhole helps keep a few of the special comforts of home at camp.

This unit also doubles as a terrific place to sit and discuss the day's hunt. It can be placed in a mudroom, but because it's pleasing to the eyes, it can be used in the den as well. If need be, the bench can be made wider or taller. In a real-guy type camp, you could use plastic or wooden boxes under the bench to store gloves and hats. See, I can be a real man, too!

Seriously, though, this is a very practical project that will provide a comfortable place to put your boots on, as well as a good spot to store your boots under the bench. I'll bet you'll enjoy having it so much that, like us, you'll wind up building more than one unit.

Hunter's Dressing & Boot Bench

Overall Size: 48 in. long, 14 in. wide 15 in. high

Tools Needed

- Table saw or handsaw
- Jigsaw
- Compound miter saw or hand miter box
- Drill
- Screw gun or driver for your drill
- Random-orbit sander

Materials

- Wood glue
- Galvanized wood screws, 2½-inch
- Wood filler or putty
- Finishing materials such as clear varnish, exterior polyurethane, or paint

Cutting List

	Part	Dimensions	Qty.	Material
A	Top seat	1 in. x 14 in. x 48 in.	1	5/4 pine
B	Bench sides	1 in. x 13¾ in. x 14 in.	2	5/4 pine
C	Side supports	1 in. x 3½ in. x 42 in.	2	5/4 pine
D	Middle support	1 in. x 3½ in. x 42 in.	1	5/4 pine
E	Inside corner supports	1 in. x 4½ in. x 4½ in.	2	5/4 pine

Note: Measurements reflect the actual thickness of dimension lumber.

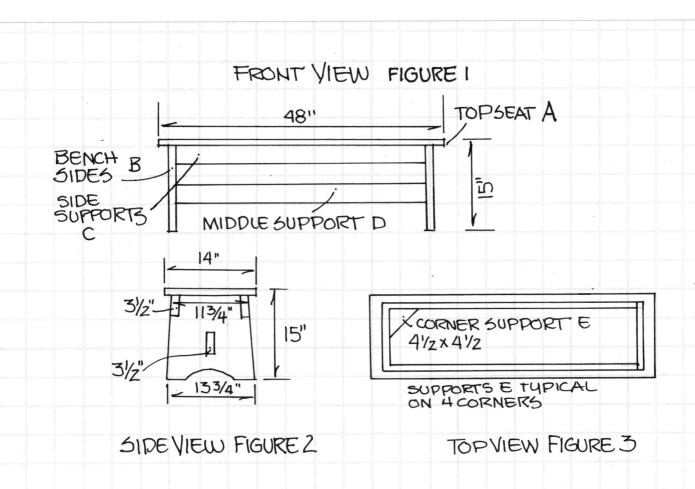

FRONT VIEW FIGURE 1

48"

TOP SEAT A

BENCH SIDES B

SIDE SUPPORTS C

MIDDLE SUPPORT D

15"

SIDE VIEW FIGURE 2

14"

3½"   11¾"

15"

3½"

13¾"

TOP VIEW FIGURE 3

CORNER SUPPORT E
4½ x 4½

SUPPORTS E TYPICAL
ON 4 CORNERS

Building the Hunter's Dressing & Boot Bench

Cut all the parts to size

1. Cut the top (A), sides (B), and supports (C, D, and E) to the lengths and widths shown in the cutting list. Use ⁵⁄₄ pine and make the cuts using a table saw or handsaw. (Note that on supports C and D, the ends can be cut at a slight angle of approximately 87 degrees if you want the sides to slant slightly as shown in the photo. For the sake of simplicity, instructions have been provided to make the cuts at 90 degrees, as shown in figure 1.)

2. Cut the foot profile on the bench sides (B) using a jigsaw. For a scaled pattern, refer to figure 2.

3. To make the four corner supports (E) cut the stock in half at 45-degree angles using a compound miter saw or hand miter box.

Assemble the bench

1. Attach the side supports (C) to the bench sides (B) using wood glue and screws. The tops of the side supports should sit flush with the top ends of the bench sides. The side supports facing the outside should be set approximately ¼ inch in from the edges of the bench sides on both ends. To prevent splitting, predrill and counter-bore the holes before driving the screws. Use two screws in each location and set the screws slightly below the outside surfaces of the bench sides.

2. Attach the middle support (D) to the bench sides (B) using wood glue and screws. The middle support should be centered on the bench sides with the top of the middle support 6½ inches from the tops of the side supports.

Hunter's Dressing & Boot Bench cont'd

Be sure to predrill and counter-bore the holes before driving the screws.

3. Attach the inside corner supports (E) in each corner using wood glue and screws. Place them so they line up with the top surfaces of the side supports and bench sides. Drill a $1/16$-inch pilot hole in the edge of each end of the corner support and screw into the side supports.

4. Attach the top seat (A) to the side support and bench side assembly. The top seat should overhang both ends approximately $1\frac{1}{2}$ inches. Use wood glue along the top surfaces of the assembly and corner supports. Use two wood screws in each corner support, screwing from the bottom into the underside of the top seat. Use three screws through the bottom of the side supports into the bottom of the bench seat—

one about 4 inches in from each end and one in the middle. Drill $1/16$-inch pilot holes with $3/8$-inch counter-bores into the same locations on the side supports. This will allow you to screw into the bottom of the bench seat and recess the heads of the screws.

Apply the finishing touches

1. Fill all the screw holes with wood filler or putty to cover the tops of the screws.

2. Sand all of the surfaces using a random-orbit sander.

3. Paint, stain, or varnish the surfaces as desired. The bench shown here has clear exterior polyurethane on the seat (A) and the lower assembly is painted with an exterior paint.

Basic Bookcase

For most sportsmen and women, having a collection of outdoor books is part and parcel of all the other hunting and fishing gear they own. For Leo and me, bookcases are an important part of our hunting camp and even of our home decor. In my house, I have seven different bookcases ranging in style from stand-alone corner units to entire wall units. At deer camp, we have one entire wall section of the TV area dedicated to an in-wall bookcase.

These bookcases not only serve to conveniently house and store our outdoor collection of books, but they also showcase them beautifully as well. And if you are like me, displaying your collection of hunting and fishing books is a big part of who you are. I pride myself in keeping all my books prominently displayed in my library, pool room, trophy room, and great room, and at deer camp as well.

I have books that I purchased—like most of you did, I'll bet—from the old Outdoor Life Book Club of the 1960s. Each month I ordered another exciting book on how to hunt deer, skin small game, or fish for trout. I read each title from cover to cover and then proudly placed it in the bookcase, which, at that time, was in my first apartment in Queens, New York. The larger the collection became the more I cherished each book.

Today I have hundreds of outdoor books in my collection, if not more, each well read and referred to many times over the years. I often catch myself just browsing through them. Each time I do, they bring a warm feeling of satisfaction to me. When I look at some of the older books, I smile because many contain information highlighted in yellow marker that, at the time, I deemed crucial advice worth noting. One such highlight came from the first outdoor book I ever read, *Shots at Whitetails* by Larry Koller. It mentioned that Koller hunted whitetail deer successfully along the famous Neversink River. At the time, the Neversink was my stomping grounds to hunt and fish.

The bookcase in this book is an easy one to build. It makes for a good first furniture project to tackle. The design included here is considered a tall bookcase, but the design can be modified easily to any height you desire. For example, if you prefer a low bookcase, build this design wider and include three or four shelves instead of six or eight. You will be amazed by what you wind up storing in the bookcase.

To add strength, the top, middle, and bottom shelves—at a minimum—should be assembled using dado joints. The middle shelves can be made adjustable to give you more flexibility in the size of objects you wind up storing on them. The design shown here has all the shelves fixed in place because it was intended to be used for a set of books of a fixed size.

Although Leo did not add trim to this project, adding face frames to the front of the sides and to the top shelf will lend it a more decorative and finished look.

For an inexpensive bookcase that can easily be stained and finished with a clear coat, choose pine. For a more upscale bookcase, you could choose a hardwood like oak or maple. If you intend to paint the bookcase to match the surrounding furniture or walls, we'd use poplar and then finish it with semi-gloss or high-gloss enamel.

This project will be a tasteful piece of furniture for your home or camp that will serve for many years as a place to house and display your cherished and valuable outdoor books.

Basic Bookcase

Tools Needed

- Table saw, circular saw, or handsaw
- Block plane
- Router with a ¼-inch rabbeting bit and a ¼-inch dado bit
- Clamp
- T-square
- Random-orbit sander or belt sander
- Hammer
- Nail set
- Wood clamp

Materials

- Wood glue
- 4d finish nails
- 1-inch brads
- Wood putty
- Finish material such as stain, lacquer, varnish, or paint

Overall Size: 33½ in. wide, 72½ in. high, 10¾ in. deep

Cutting List

	Part	Dimensions	Qty.	Material
A	Top shelf	¾ in. x 10¾ in. x 33½ in.	1	Pine
B	Shelves	¾ in. x 10½ in. x 31 in.	6	Pine
C	Sides	¾ in. x 10¾ in. x 72 in.	2	Pine
D	Bottom base	¾ in. x 2½ in. x 30½ in.	1	Pine
E	Back	¼ in. x 30¾ in. x 72 in.	1	Luan mahogany plywood

Note: Measurements reflect the actual thickness of dimension lumber.

Basic Bookcase cont'd

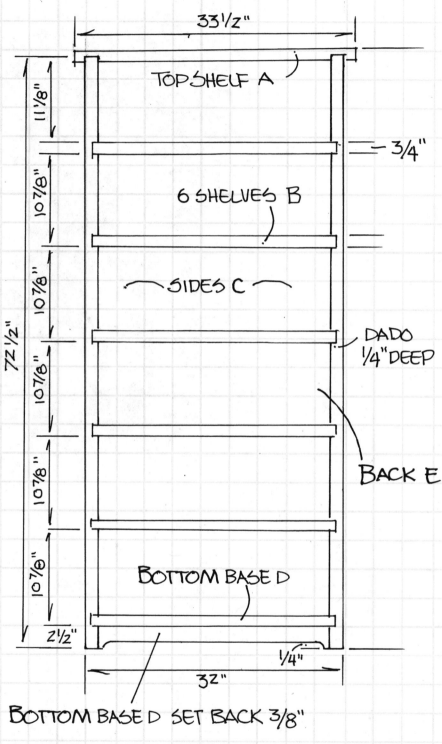

33½"

TOP SHELF A

11⅛"

3/4"

6 SHELVES B

10⅞"

SIDES C

10⅞"

72½"

DADO
¼" DEEP

10⅞"

BACK E

10⅞"

BOTTOM BASE D

10⅞"

2½"

¼"

32"

BOTTOM BASE D SET BACK 3/8"

FRONT VIEW   FIGURE 1

Building the Basic Bookcase

Cut all the parts to size

1. Measure and cut all the pieces (A, B, C, D, and E) to the sizes shown in the cutting list. A table saw will give you cuts that are straight and square, but a circular saw or handsaw can be used instead. If you do not have access to a table saw, many local lumberyards and home centers will make the cuts for you at a small charge.
2. Make sure all edges are smooth and square. If you made the cuts with a handsaw, use a block plane to clean up the cuts.

Cut the joinery

1. Lay out and cut the rabbet joints on the top (A) and side pieces (C). This can be done in several different ways depending on the tools you have. The most accurate tool to use is a router with a $\frac{3}{4}$-inch dado bit and a side guide. Set the depth of the router bit to be $\frac{1}{4}$ inch deep.
2. Lay out the top shelf on a flat surface. Set the guide to cut a dado $\frac{3}{4}$ inch in from each end. Carefully run the router across each end of the board.
3. Lay the sides on a flat surface side by side. Mark the locations of the dado cuts, as shown in figure 1, using a T-square. Use a clamp at both ends to secure the stock side by side. Clamp a scrap of wood, approximately $\frac{1}{2}$ inch x 1 inch with a straight edge, in place as a guide for the router. Before clamping the guide in place, position it so that the router bit lines up in the desired location for the dado joint. Carefully run the router across the boards and repeat this same procedure for the remaining dado cuts on the side pieces.

Assemble the parts

1. Lay out both side pieces (C) on end about 32 inches apart and place a drop of wood glue in the dado joints. To prevent the excess glue from running out the sides onto the shelves, use only a modest amount of glue.
2. Place all of the shelves (B) in between the dado joints. Make sure that the front edges of the shelves are flush with the front edge of the side pieces. Using three 4d finish nails for each end, nail through the side board into the shelf ends. Repeat the same process for the other side and the remaining shelves.
3. Set the bottom base (D) below the bottom shelf and inset $\frac{3}{8}$ inch from the front edge. Attach it using 4d finish nails driven in from the side and from the top of the bottom shelf.
4. Set the top shelf (A) on the top ends of the sides so that the back edge is flush with the back edge of the side pieces. Use wood glue and three 4d finish nails driven in from the top to secure it in place.
5. Lay the assembled bookcase on its front edge so that the rear edges are accessible. Using a router with a dado bit set at a depth of $\frac{1}{4}$ inch, run the router around the entire inside edge of the top and sides to create a rabbet for the back to sit in.
6. Apply wood glue to the rabbets around the top and sides. Also place a line of glue on the rear edge of each shelf. Position the back piece (E) in between the rabbet joints and on the shelf edges. Using 1-inch brads, nail the back piece to the edges. Space the brads about 8 inches apart along the rabbet joint and across the back of each shelf.

Apply the finishing touches

1. Use a clean, wet cloth to wipe off any excess glue around the joints.
2. Set all the finish nails below the surface of the wood using a nail set.
3. Fill all visible holes with wood putty or filler.
4. Sand the exposed surface using a random-orbit sander.
5. Stain, lacquer, varnish, or paint the bookcase as you see fit. For a more rustic look, you can even leave the bookcase unfinished and let it gray with age.

Outdoorsman's Picture Frame

Nothing enhances a deer camp, cabin, or home more than a wildlife print in a rustic frame—especially a frame you built yourself. I have been buying and collecting signed and numbered wildlife and Native American prints for more than twenty-five years. They adorn the walls of my home, office, and deer cabin. I have a collection that includes works by renowned wildlife artists Robert Bateman, Terry Redlin, Charles Denault, Hayden Lambson, and many others. But since all my homes are decorated in a Southwestern theme, my absolute favorite artist is Ken Schmidt.

Ken is a full-time artist from upstate New York. Working mainly in watercolors and pencil, Ken has developed his own unique style portraying the Native American, the mountain man, and the cowboy. Ken travels the country photographing live models and scenery, which he uses as the subjects and settings for his paintings and drawings.

Ken's work has been featured on the covers of nationally known magazines such as *Art of the West*, *Midwest Art*, and *Wild West*. Recently, his artwork has captured a more international audience and has been shown in Europe. Ken's personal attention to detail and realism breathe life into his paintings, allowing collectors like me to feel and experience the rugged existence that his subjects endured. In a recent conversation I had with Ken, he told me, "When I paint, I'm communicating with the subjects, putting their thoughts into the portrait. It's almost like they're telling me what they've done in their lives. I get lost, drawn into the paintings, just like I hope people who look at them do." If you are interested in seeing more of Ken's amazing artwork visit his Web site at www.lonefeatherstudio.com.

Only a dedicated outdoorsman understands the unique relationship that exists between outdoorsmen and women and their wildlife prints. They tell the world who we are and what our lifestyle is all about. They are part and parcel of the connection to our history, heritage, sport, and wildlife we all hold so dear.

Back in the late 1980s another talented wildlife artist and longtime friend Adriano Manocchia suggested that we partner together to create a signed and numbered wildlife print. After a lot of discussion, I provided Adriano a detailed description of a scene from one of my hunting areas known as the "The Bowl" that included a hunter and a buck. That print was called *Whitetail Strategies "Teamwork"* because it was about two hunters rattling in a trophy-class buck. It is signed by both the artist Adriano Manocchia and me. Leo decided to mount this print in the frame that he designed and created for this book. The print is available at www.woodsnwater.tv.

This frame will make any print, wildlife or otherwise, a real eye-catcher. It is also surprisingly simple to build. As Leo explained, "The frame and print hang in my office, and when days get a bit rough at work, I stare at it for a few minutes. It helps me drift off to deer-hunting memories—deer hunting is my true joy in life—and the pursuit of a wily ol' buck who has outsmarted all deer hunters that have tried to take him on his own turf. The hunter in the stand was from a photo taken on my brother Ralph's property. The stand is called 'four-point' because the first buck taken from it was a buck that had a high, wide, four-point rack with a 20-inch spread! Every time I look at the print I get excited. This print is what gave me the desire and motivation to write this book."

This frame was built to hold a wildlife print in a mat that measures 18 inches x 24 inches, which is a standard size. It's a simple matter to adjust the measurements if your print or original oil painting is smaller or larger. If the frame is made smaller, I would suggest adjusting the width of the actual frame pieces to 2¹/₄ inches or smaller.

We used red oak, one of our favorite woods, for this project. You can finish it with a clear coat of polyurethane or lacquer if you are looking for the natural oak color. Or you can easily stain it and then finish it with a clear coat to match the decor of your room. Other woods that enhance the look of this frame are cedar, knotty pine, or cherry.

Building this frame will help save you a lot of money when purchasing wildlife prints, too. Instead of having to buy the prints already framed, you can buy them unframed and save at least 50 to 75 percent off the retail purchase cost. That means you can buy many more wildlife prints for your collection. The materials you need to buy to build this frame are not going to break the bank either.

This is one of our favorite projects because of the simplicity of building it, the handsomeness it adds to any space, and the savings it provides when collecting prints. It also gets the most compliments from everyone who sees it. Build this frame as one of your first projects and the satisfaction you get from it will motivate you to move on to some of the more challenging projects in this book.

Outdoorsman's Picture Frame

Overall Size: 28½ in. long, 22½ in. wide

Tools Needed

- Table saw, compound miter saw, or hand miter box
- Hammer
- Router with a ¼-inch round-over bit and a ¼-inch veining bit
- Wood file
- Wood clamps

Materials

- Wood glue
- ⅜-inch corrugated joint fasteners
- 1-inch brads
- 120-grain sandpaper
- Finishing materials: polyurethane, lacquer, or stain
- ⅛-inch glass or Plexiglas, 18 inches x 24 inches
- Framer's points
- Picture frame wire and eyelets

Cutting List

	Part	Dimensions	Qty.	Material
A	Frame rails	¾ in. x 2¼ in. x 24 in.	2	Red oak
B	Frame stiles	¾ in. x 2¼ in. x 22½ in.	2	Red oak
C	Front trim rail	½ in. x 1 in. x 26½ in.	2	Red oak
D	Front trim stiles	½ in. x 1 in. x 17⅜ in.	2	Red oak
E	Backing	⅛ in. x 18 in. x 24 in.	1	Luan mahogany

Note: Measurements reflect the actual thickness of dimension lumber.

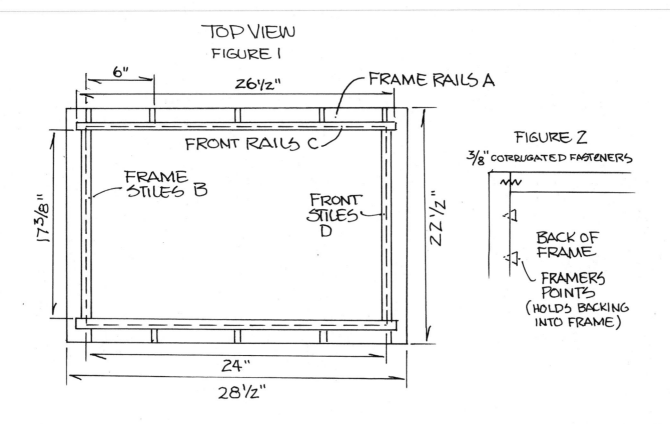

TOP VIEW
FIGURE I

FRAME RAILS A

6"   26½"

FRONT RAILS C

FRAME STILES B

FRONT STILES D

17⅜"   22½"

24"

28½"

FIGURE 2
⅜" CORRUGATED FASTENERS

BACK OF FRAME

FRAMERS POINTS
(HOLDS BACKING INTO FRAME)

Building the Outdoorsman's Picture Frame

Prepare and assemble the frame parts

1. Measure and cut all the pieces (A, B, C, D, and E) to the sizes shown in the cutting list. For the cleanest cuts, use a table saw or a compound miter saw. A handsaw can be used as well, but you'll want to clean up the rough edges with a block plane.

2. Use a router with a ¼-inch round-over bit to profile the edges of the front trim rails (C) and stiles (D).

3. Lay out the two frame stiles (B) against a flat work surface about 24 inches apart. Then lay the frame rails (A) in between the two frame stiles (B), as shown in figure 1.

4. Put a thin layer of glue at the four corners where the stiles meet the rails.

5. To make sure your frame corners are square, test their alignment against a square or measure the frame's diagonals (from corner to corner). When the diagonals are equal, the frame is square. Place wood clamps on the top

and bottom of each stile and tighten them so that the stiles are snug against the rails. Then nail a ⅜-inch corrugated joint fastener in each corner to ensure that the joint is tight, as shown in figure 2. Recheck the assembly for squareness, and then allow the glue to dry for several hours before removing the clamps.

Add the front stiles

1. Using a router outfitted with a ¼-inch round-over bit, profile the outside edges of the picture frame.

2. Use a wood file to mill a groove approximately every 2 inches along the entire outside edge of the frame. Make grooves 2 inches long and ¼-inch wide.

3. Using the router with a ¼-inch veining bit, cut grooves in the top (A) and bottom (B) rails at the locations as shown in figure 1.

4. Lay one of the front trim rails (C) on the top rail (A) so that it overhangs ⅜ inch beyond the in-

Outdoorsman's Picture Frame cont'd

side edge (this front trim piece is what will hold the glass and artwork in the frame). Nail the front trim to the rail using four 1-inch brads. Repeat this step for the second front trim rail on the bottom.

5. Lay one of the front trim stiles (D) in between the top and bottom rails (C) so that it overhangs the inside edge by $3/8$ inch. Nail the trim piece to the stile using four 1-inch brads. Repeat this step for the second front trim stile on the other side.

6. Smooth all the surfaces using 120-grain sandpaper and apply the finish of your choice..

Frame your print or picture

1. Turn the frame over so that the front is face-down on a flat surface.

2. Place the glass or Plexiglas inside the frame opening.

3. Lay your favorite print or picture inside the frame on the glass.

4. Place the backing (E) on top of the print.

5. Secure it in place by using three to four framer's points along the frame rails and stiles. Bang the framer's points into the sides of rails and stiles using a small hammer, making sure that they are pressing against the backing.

6. Secure the eyelets for the hanging wire about 5 inches down from the top of the frame on each of the frame stiles.

7. Twist the wire into each of the eyelets so that there is about 1 inch of slack in the wire.

CHAPTER 5

Sheds and Storage

- Firewood Storage Shed
- Garbage Bin Container
- Firewood Box
- Tool and Garden Shed
- Workbench

Firewood Storage Shed

In light of rising fuel costs, this 8-foot-wide x 7-foot-high firewood shed came just in time this past season at our camp. We usually turn the furnace on and forget about the heat and the heating oil bills, but not this year. We spent a lot of time at the cabin and used nothing but wood to keep us warm, relying on the burner to keep the pipes from freezing only when we weren't there.

There is no denying the fact that cutting, stacking, and storing firewood—to say nothing of stoking the fire—is a bit more work, but it is great exercise. Nothing, though, is as important as having the wood stored in an adequate location. The wood has to be absolutely dried out to keep a good fire going. Not only is wet wood harder and less efficient to burn, but it also produces more creosote, which creates a potential fire hazard in the stack.

One of the things to keep in mind as you prepare to burn wood is the process used to dry it out. For best results, wood should be dried outdoors for at least one year, then for another year in a wood shed, with only a week's supply dried indoors just before it is used. This means that to solve the problem of storing and seasoning wood, the serious wood burner should think about building a permanent, freestanding wood shed. The shed keeps insects and dirt to a minimum, allowing the wood to dry under ideal conditions. We built our shed close to our back door, so it's convenient to get at the wood.

This shed easily holds three to four cords of wood and provides a great place to season the wood while keeping it very dry. If you need to build a shed that is larger or smaller, you can still use the basic construction techniques described here.

I recommend using T-111 for your siding. It is relatively inexpensive in comparison to other wood siding and accepts stain of any color well. If you really want to save some money, you can also make use of old siding that you might have lying around.

Firewood Storage Shed

Overall size: 100 in. long, 48 in. wide, 90 in. high

Tools Needed

- Table saw, circular saw, or handsaw
- Hammer
- Tape measure
- T-square or combination square
- Level
- Staple gun
- Utility knife
- Chalk line
- Jigsaw
- Screwdriver or drill with a driver bit
- Wood clamps
- Clamps

Materials

- Hot-dipped galvanized nails: sizes 16d, 10d, 8d, 6d
- Roofing nails: sizes $\frac{1}{2}$ inch and $1\frac{3}{4}$ inch
- $1\frac{1}{2}$-inch siding nails
- Finish nails: sizes 6d, 4d, 2d
- Asphalt roofing shingles
- #15 rolled asphalt paper
- Staples
- Two 4-foot x 16-inch flat vents
- White metal roof edging—three 10-foot lengths
- Exterior-grade finish of your choice
- Roofing cement

Cutting List

	Part	Dimensions	Qty.	Material
A	Railroad ties	$5\frac{1}{2}$ in. x $5\frac{1}{2}$ in. x 48 in.	3	Pressure-treated ACQ
B	Floor joists	$1\frac{1}{2}$ in. x $5\frac{1}{2}$ in. x 94 in.	4	Pressure-treated ACQ
C	Flooring	$\frac{3}{4}$ in. x 48 in. x 94 in.	1	Pressure-treated ACQ plywood
D	Front/rear/side wall studs	$1\frac{1}{2}$ in. x $2\frac{1}{2}$ in. x 72 in.	15	Douglas fir
E	Rear/front wall plates	$1\frac{1}{2}$ in. x $2\frac{1}{2}$ in. x 94 in.	5	Douglas fir
F	Side wall plates	$1\frac{1}{2}$ in. x $2\frac{1}{2}$ in. x 48 in.	4	Douglas fir
G	Top front angles	$1\frac{1}{2}$ in. x $2\frac{1}{2}$ in. x 14 in.	2	Douglas fir
H	Rear roof rafters	$1\frac{1}{2}$ in. x $3\frac{1}{2}$ in. x 45 in.	7	Douglas fir
I	Front roof rafters	$1\frac{1}{2}$ in. x $3\frac{1}{2}$ in. x 31 in.	7	Douglas fir
J	Fascia trim	$\frac{3}{4}$ in. x $4\frac{1}{2}$ in. x 96 in.	2	Cedar
K	Side wall panels	$\frac{5}{8}$ in. x $47\frac{5}{8}$ in. x 92 in.	2	Exterior T-111 siding
L	Rear wall panels	$\frac{5}{8}$ in. x $47\frac{5}{8}$ in. x 80 in.	2	Exterior T-111 siding

Firewood Storage Shed cont'd

Part		Dimensions	Qty.	Material
M	Roof plywood, front	¾ in. x 31 in. x 96 in.	1	Pressure-treated ACQ
N	Roof plywood, rear	¾ in. x 45 in. x 96 in.	1	Pressure-treated ACQ
O	Front wall panels	⅝ in. x 24 in. x 80 in.	2	Exterior T-111 siding
P	Frame top trim	¾ in. x 3½ in. x 56 in.	1	Cedar
Q	Frame angle trim	¾ in. x 3½ in. x 14 in.	1	Cedar
R	Frame side trim	¾ in. x 3½ in. x 68 in.	2	Cedar
S	Corner trim	¼ in. x 1 in. x 80 in.	8	Cedar

Note: Measurements reflect the actual thickness of dimension lumber.

BOTTOM VIEW FIGURE 1

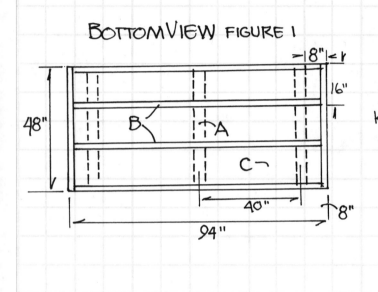

REAR VIEW FIGURE 3

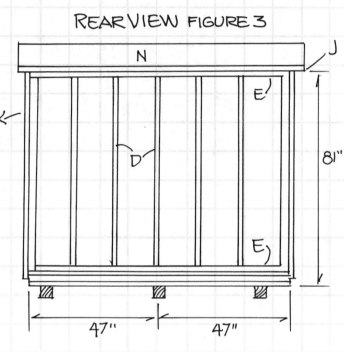

FRONT VIEW FIGURE 2

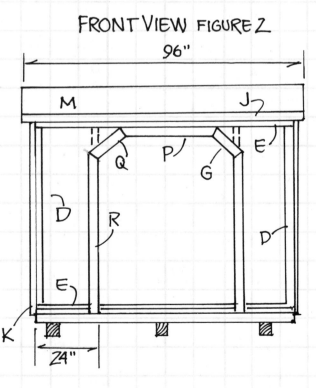

SIDE VIEW FIGURE 4

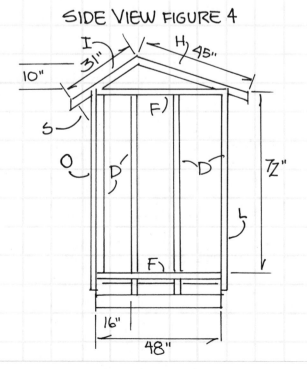

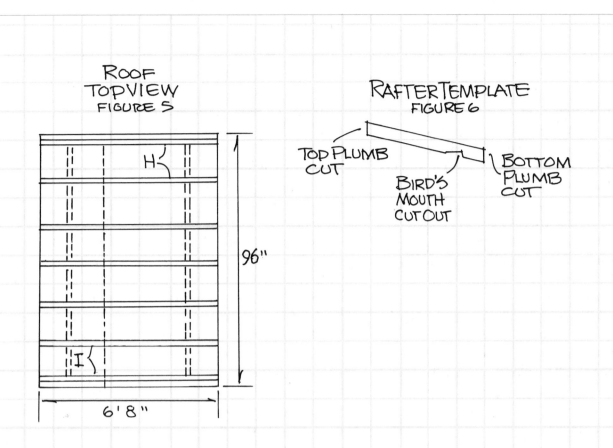

ROOF
TOPVIEW
FIGURE 5

RAFTER TEMPLATE
FIGURE 6

TOP PLUMB CUT

BIRD'S MOUTH CUT OUT

BOTTOM PLUMB CUT

96"

6'8"

Building the Firewood Storage Shed

Construct the floor platform

1. Measure and cut the railroad ties (A), floor joists (B), and plywood flooring (C) as shown in the cutting list. If you buy a single sheet of 4-foot x 8-foot plywood for the flooring, you shouldn't have to cut it at all.

2. Lay out the three railroad ties (A) on the flat surface where you plan for the building to sit. Space them approximately 40 inches apart.

3. Position the four floor joists (B) on top of the railroad ties (A). Two of the joists should align with the ends of the railroad ties (A) and the other two should be placed at intervals of 16 inches on center. Secure the joists to the railroad ties by toenailing 8d nails through the joists and into the railroad ties.

4. Place the flooring (C) on top of the platform box you just assembled, aligning the outside edges of the flooring with the outside edges of the joists. Nail the plywood to each joist using 8d nails spaced about 8 inches apart.

Construct the front and rear walls

1. Measure and cut the wall studs and plates (D, E, and F) as shown in the cutting list and in figures 2 and 3.

2. Face-nail two of the top plates (E) side by side using 10d nails. This piece will be used as your top front plate.

3. Lay out the top front plate assembly and bottom front wall plates (E) on edge. Measure and mark the location of the wall studs on each of these plates using a square. Place the four front wall studs (D) in place—one at each end of the plates and the other two between them at intervals of 24 inches from each end. Nail through the plates using two 16d nails into the end of each stud.

4. Stand up the assembled front wall frame and place it on top of the floor platform so that its outside edge is flush with the front edge of the floor. Make sure that the doubled-up top plate is indeed on the top of the wall. Nail through

Firewood Storage Shed cont'd

the bottom front wall plate (E) and floor into the front joist (B) using six 16d nails.

5. Use a handsaw to cut out the front bottom wall plate from the front opening.

6. Cut the top front angles (G) and then toenail them into place on the studs using 10d nails.

7. Build the rear wall. Lay out the top and bottom rear wall plates (E) on edge and mark out the stud locations. Place two rear wall studs (D) at both ends of the wall plates and the other five equally spaced at locations between (E), then nail them in place using two 16d nails in each stud end.

8. Stand the assembled rear wall frame upright and place it atop the rear floor platform so that its outside edge is flush with the edge of the floor. Nail through the bottom rear wall plate (E) and flooring (C) into the rear joist (B) using six 16d nails.

Frame the side walls

1. Lay out the top and bottom side wall plates (F) on edge. Measure and mark the location of the wall studs on these plates, as shown in figure 4. Place the two rear wall studs (D) at the locations shown (approximately 16 inches apart on center) and nail them together with two 16d nails in each stud end.

2. Raise the assembled sidewall frame upright and place it on top of the side floor platform so that its outside edge is flush with the edge of the flooring. Drive six 16d nails through the bottom side wall plate (F) and flooring (C).

3. Repeat steps 1 and 2 for the other side.

Construct the roof

Note: On the roof shown in this design, the roof ridge is off center—it is closer to the front wall. You could also build the shed with the roof ridge centered front to back. Refer to the roof rafter template shown in figure 6 for an understanding of the terms discussed below.

1. Use a square to mark the locations of roof rafters along the top front and rear wall plates.

Position them 16 inches apart on center.

2. Measure and cut the rafters. To position the rafters, you'll probably need the help of friend. At the very least, you'll need a few clamps to hold parts in position as you mark them. Place the front roof rafter (I) on top of the front wall so that it overhangs the front by approximately 10 inches and the ridge end of the rafter is raised 10 inches above the side wall plate. To mark out the plumb cuts on the ends of the rafters, place a level against each rafter. Make sure it reads level in the vertical direction and then mark the rafter for the bottom cut. Repeat the same process to determine the top plumb cut.

3. With the rafter still in position, mark the location of the bird's mouth—both its plumb cut and its level one.

4. Use a handsaw or circular saw to make all of the plumb cuts and form the bird's mouth cut.

5. Temporarily support the front rafter in place by nailing a 2x4 support from the top plumb cut to the side wall plate.

6. Repeat the same procedure described in steps 2, 3, and 4 above to mark and cut the rear roof rafter (H).

7. Use the front and rear roof rafters as a pattern to make the remaining six sets of rafters.

8. Lay the front and rear roof rafters at one end of the shed side walls. You will need a helper to hold them in place. Toenail two 8d nails through the rafters and into the top wall plate at the bird's mouth locations.

9. Nail the top, plumb-cut ends of the front and rear rafters together by toenailing two 8d nails through each into the other.

10. Repeat steps 8 and 9 for the remaining six sets of rafters, placing them on the 16-inch centers you marked out in step 1 above.

11. Measure and cut the plywood roof pieces (M) and (N) as shown in the cutting list.

12. Place the plywood for the front side of the roof (M) on top of the front roof rafters so that it overhangs evenly on the front and top wall edges. Nail the plywood in place on the rafters

using 6d nails. Nails should be placed approximately 8 inches apart along each of the rafters.

13. Place the roof plywood for the rear side of the roof (N) on topo of the rear roof rafters. Nail it in place into the rafters using 6d nails. Nails should be place approximately 8 inches apart along each of the rafters.

Apply roof shingles

1. Apply asphalt building paper starting from the bottom of the roof and working your way up, overlapping the lower paper with the paper above it. Staple the building paper in place with a staple gun. You can install white metal-roof edging to finish off the plywood roof edges. Measure and cut the pieces and install them on the edges using ½-inch roofing nails.

2. Start on the rear roof and snap a chalk line 11½ inches up from the rear roof edge.

3. Trim off one half (6 inches) of the end tab of a shingle using a utility knife and straightedge.

4. Position the shingle upside-down, so the tabs are on the chalk line and the half-tab overhangs the roof edge by ¾-inch. Fasten the shingle with four 1¾ inch roofing nails, spaced about 3½ inches up from the bottom edge: drive one below each tab, one 2 inches in from the edge, and another 1 inch from the inside edge. To avoid tearing the shingle, drive the nails straight and set the heads just flush to the shingle.

5. Use full shingles for the remainder of the starter course, placing them upside down and butting their edges together. Trim the last shingle so it overhangs the edge by ½ inch.

6. Install the first course of shingles, starting with a full shingle. Position the tabs down and align the shingle edges with those in the starter course. Drive four nails into each shingle, trimming the last shingle to match the starter course.

7. Snap a chalk line on the building paper. Position the line 17 inches up from the bottom edge of the first course, resulting in a 5-inch exposure for each course.

8. Begin the second course with a full shingle, but overhang the end of the first course by half of a tab. Begin the third course by overhanging a full tab, then one and a half tabs for the fourth course. Start the fifth course with a full shingle aligned with the first course, maintaining a 5-inch exposure.

9. Continue this procedure until the shingles are parallel to the top ridge, and then trim off the top course at the ridge.

10. Repeat the same procedure to shingle the remaining side of the roof. Overlap the roof ridge with the top course of shingles and nail them to the outer roof side. Make sure they don't overlap by more than 4½ inches.

11. Cut ridge caps from standard shingle tabs: taper each tab along the side edges, starting from the tops of the slots and cutting up to the top edges. Cut three caps from each shingle. You will need one cap for every 5 inches of ridge.

12. Snap a chalk line 6 inches from the ridge across the shingles. Starting at the gable ends, install the caps by bending them over the ridge and aligning one side with the chalk line. Fasten each cap with one nail on each roof side, 5 inches from the finished (exposed) edge and 1 inch from the side edge. Fasten the last shingle with a nail at each corner, and then cover the nail heads with roofing cement.

13. Trim the overhanging shingles along the gable ends. Snap chalk lines along the gable ends, ⅜ inch from the edges, and trim the shingles at the lines. Cover any exposed nails with roofing cement.

14. Secure the fascia trim (J) on the ends of the roof rafters (front and rear) using 8d finish nails into the ends.

Wrap the shed in siding

1. Measure and cut the side, rear, and front wall panels (K, L, and O), as shown in the cutting list.

2. Place one of the side wall panels (K) against

Firewood Storage Shed cont'd

the side wall so that the edges are flush with the rear and front walls. Mark the angles of the roof rafters along the top piece of the siding and cut the angles using a jigsaw. Then secure the panel to the side wall studs using 1½-inch siding nails. Repeat this same procedure to attach the siding to the other wall.

3. Place one of the rear wall panels (L) against the rear wall so that one edge is flush to the edge of the sidewall panel. Secure it to the rear wall studs using 1½-inch siding nails. Repeat this same procedure for the other rear wall panel.

4. Place one of the front wall panels (O) against the front wall with one edge flush to the edge of the side wall siding. Secure it to the front wall studs using 1½-inch siding nails. Repeat this same procedure for the other front wall panel.

5. Using a jigsaw, cut two pieces of siding to match the top frame angle and nail it in place on both sides of the opening. You should be able to use scraps from the side wall panels to make up these pieces.

Apply the finishing touches

1. Measure and cut the remaining pieces (P, Q, R, and S) as shown in the cutting list.

2. Trim out the doorframe using the doorframe top (P), angle (Q), and side (R) trim pieces. Secure them to the wall studs using 6d finish nails.

3. Add corner trim pieces (S) to the four corners and secure them in place using 2d finish nails.

4. Finish the exterior surfaces with an exterior stain or paint. Although it's not really necessary, you may want to stain or paint the interior surfaces. If so, use an exterior grade of stain or latex paint.

5. Mark out the location of the flat vent just below the roof ridge on one of the gable ends. Use a jigsaw to cut an opening close to the roof ridge. Attach the vent to the siding using wood screws. Repeat the same steps to install the vent on the other side.

Garbage Bin Container

Several years ago, we lived about six miles from where I live now. We had a wonderful little house on four acres that was bordered by a large abandoned farm and surrounded by thousands of acres of mountainous land. It was the perfect setting for us to see all kinds of wildlife from our den window. Each and every day we saw numerous wild turkey, deer, and even black bear in the small field alongside our house.

One evening my wife Kate and I heard a ruckus in the yard, turned on the floodlights, and watched in total amazement as a large black bear boar shredded to pieces a full-size McKenzie elk target. We then watched as he tore apart "The Block™" archery target as well. Both targets were about 50 yards from our home and in a direct line to where our garbage containers were stored. Once he finished with the targets, he headed straight for our garbage cans. Maybe he thought the elk was going to dine on the garbage cans and that is why he decided to kill the poor thing!

Because we had bear problems before, our garbage containers were made from heavy steel and had large, heavy-duty spring-locking lids. We continued to watch in shock as the big black bear boar took one handle of the first can in his mouth and lifted the container full of garbage completely off the ground! Without any hesitation he made a perfect golf swing at the second can, sending it flying toward the woods. Tiger Woods would have been proud of his form.

Next, he trotted off toward the woods with the handle of the first can still tightly gripped in his mouth. When he reached the second can, now lying on its side, he dropped the first can from his mouth, picked up the second can, and ran into the woods carrying it as if it were an empty paper cup. He quickly returned from the wood lot, grabbed the remaining garbage container, and disappeared into the woods.

The next day we searched the woods for the cans. We were sure we would find them within 50 yards of the wood line. Once again the power and determination of this bear surprised us—we located the cans, completely demolished, about 100 yards from our house. The covers were ripped off and bent; one can was flattened and almost bent in half; the other can was less damaged but still in bad shape. To see just how strong this bear was, I tried to straighten out the lids. Despite using all my strength, I couldn't do it.

While this incident was out of the norm for the local bears that regularly tried to steal our garbage containers, it was dramatic enough for us to realize that we had to do something to prevent a bear of this size, strength, and foul attitude from returning to our home again and again. It was time to buy two more steel cans and enclose them in a garbage bin built sturdily enough to deter even the most stubborn bear.

To the rescue came Leo Somma. The plans for the Garbage Bin Container are from the original design of the unit built by Leo to keep the bears from scattering my trash all over the woods behind my house. While I did have one bear that pushed the door in, he couldn't get the cans out. We ended that problem by making the door a little sturdier.

Even if you don't have bear problems like I did, you probably have pesky critters opening and eating your trash and leaving a mess. If that's the case, this project is for you. It will keep even the cleverest raccoon, coyote, skunk, or other bandit from making your garbage his midnight smorgasbord. The very first time you don't have to sweep or scrape up stinky garbage left behind by a critter raiding your trash can, you'll be glad you built it.

Garbage Bin Container

Overall Size: 62 in. long, 32 in. wide, 42 in. high

Tools Needed

- Table saw, circular saw, or handsaw
- Tape measure
- Hammer
- Screwdriver
- Drill and ¼-inch bit
- Jigsaw
- Level

Materials

- Wood glue
- Hot-dipped galvanized nails—sizes 16d, 6d
- 1½-inch siding nails
- Four 3-inch hasp hinges with screws (for the doors)
- Three 4-inch hinges with screws (for the top cover)
- Two door latches with screws
- 4d finish nails
- Exterior-grade latex stain

Cutting List

	Part	Dimensions	Qty.	Material
A	Floor supports	3½ in. x 3½ in. x 30 in.	3	Pressure-treated ACQ
B	Floor platform	¾ in. x 30 in. x 60 in.	1	Pressure-treated ACQ Plywood
C	Rear wall studs	1½ in. x 2½ in. x 35 in.	4	Douglas fir
D	Rear/front wall supports	1½ in. x 2½ in. x 60 in.	4	Douglas fir
E	Front wall studs	1½ in. x 2½ in. x 33 in.	3	Douglas fir
F	Side wall supports	1½ in. x 2½ in. x 26 in.	2	Douglas fir
G	Top frame, long	1½ in. x 2½ in. x 62 in.	2	Douglas fir
H	Top frame, short	1½ in. x 2½ in. x 26 in.	3	Douglas fir
I	Rear siding	⅝ in. x 39½ in. x 61¼ in.	1	Exterior T-111 siding
J	Front siding	⅝ in. x 37½ in. x 61¼ in.	1	Exterior T-111 siding

Garbage Bin Container cont'd

Part		Dimensions	Qty.	Material
K	Side siding	$\frac{5}{8}$ in. x 40 in. x 30 in.	2	Exterior T-111 siding
L	Top cover	$\frac{5}{8}$ in. x 31 in. x 62 in.	1	Exterior T-111 siding
M	Doorframe, long	$1\frac{1}{2}$ in. x $2\frac{1}{2}$ in. x $32\frac{3}{4}$ in.	4	Douglas fir
N	Doorframe, short	$1\frac{1}{2}$ in. x $2\frac{1}{2}$ in. x $21\frac{3}{4}$ in.	4	Douglas fir
O	Corner trim	$\frac{1}{4}$ in.x $1\frac{1}{4}$ in.x 38 in.	8	Pine

Note: Measurements reflect the actual thickness of dimension lumber.

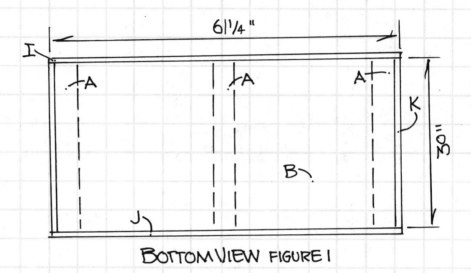

BOTTOM VIEW FIGURE 1

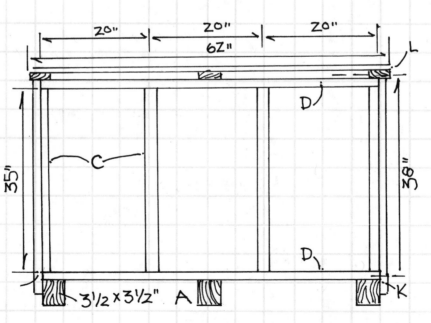

REAR VIEW FIGURE 2

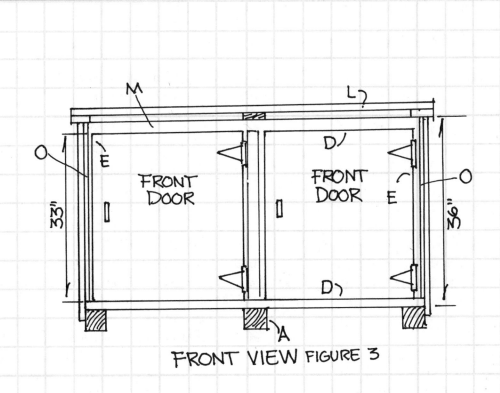

FRONT VIEW FIGURE 3

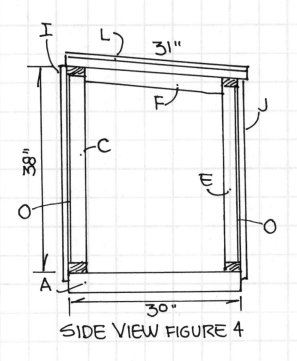

SIDE VIEW FIGURE 4

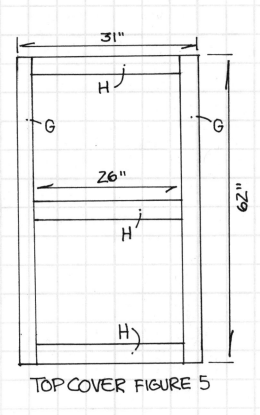

TOP COVER FIGURE 5

Garbage Bin Container cont'd

Building the Garbage Bin Container

Construct the floor platform

1. Use a table saw, circular saw, or handsaw to cut the floor supports (A) and floor platform (B) to the sizes shown in cutting list.
2. Lay out the three floor supports (A) on your work surface. Place them on edge—two of them approximately 60 inches apart and one in the middle, as shown in figure 1.
3. Place the floor platform (B) on top of the three floor supports (A). Make sure that the edges of the plywood are flush with the end supports and front. Secure the platform to the supports using wood glue and 6d galvanized nails. Nail at 8-inch centers along the floor supports.

Construct the rear, front, and side walls

1. Measure and cut the rear wall studs (C), the rear and front wall supports (D), and front wall studs (E) to the sizes shown in the cutting list.
2. Lay out two of the rear wall supports (D) on edge and approximately 36 inches apart. Place four of the rear wall studs (C) in between the supports—two at each end and the other two equally spaced between the ends. Secure the studs in place by nailing two 10d nails through the supports and into each end of the wall studs.
3. Position two of the front wall supports (D) on edge approximately 33 inches apart. Place three of the front wall studs (E) in between the supports—two at each end and the other one in the middle. Secure in place as in step 2 above.
4. Place the rear wall structure on top of the rear of the floor platform. Secure it to the platform by nailing 16d nails through the bottom wall support and the platform and into the bottom floor supports.
5. Repeat step 4 to install the front wall support structure.
6. Cut and place the end siding (K) flush to the ends of the front and rear wall studs. Trace the roof angle from front to back and make the cut using a jigsaw or circular saw. The top of the siding should be flush with the top of the rear and front wall corner studs. Secure it in place by nailing 1½-inch siding nails along the corner rear wall stud, the corner front wall stud, and the end floor support. Repeat this same procedure to install the siding on the other end.
7. Place one of the side wall supports (F) against the top of the side wall and mark the angle of the cut to be made on both ends of the wall support. Cut the angle with a circular saw or handsaw. Place the support flush with the top of the siding. Secure the side wall support to the corner studs by toenailing 8d nails into the ends. Secure the siding in place by nailing 1½-inch siding nails into the side wall support. Repeat this same procedure for the opposite side.
8. Cut and place the rear siding (I) against the rear wall support structure and secure it in place by using 1½-inch siding nails driven into the studs. Make sure that the rear siding is flush with the top of the rear wall support.
9. Repeat step 8 for the front siding (J). (Note: the front siding will be cut into two separate doors, as described later)

Make the top cover

1. Measure and cut parts G, H, and L. Lay out the top frame pieces (G) and (H) as shown in figure 5. Assemble the top frame using 16d nails driven into each corner and through the middle support.
2. Place the top cover (L) in place on top of the top frame. Make sure that the siding is flush with the outside edges of the frame and secure it to the frame using 1½-inch siding nails. Nails should be spaced along the edges on 8-inch centers.
3. The back of the top cover should be flush with the rear siding but overhang the sides and front by approximately 1 inch. Attach the top cover to the bin by installing three 4-inch hinges into the rear of the top cover and into

Tool and Garden Shed

Tools Needed

- Table saw or handsaw
- Hammer
- Level
- Tape measure
- Compound miter saw or circular saw
- T-square or combination square
- Screwdriver or driver bit for your drill
- Drill and set of bits

Materials

- Hot-dipped galvanized nails: sizes 16d, 10d, 8d, and 6d
- Siding nails, 1½-inch
- Finish nails, 1½-inch
- Hinges, 4-inch
- Doorknob set
- Exterior-grade latex stain or paint
- Four 8-inch x 8-inch x 16-inch cinder blocks (may substitute railroad ties)
- Nails and tool hooks of various sizes.

Overall Size: 72 in. long, 30 in. wide, 94 in. high

Cutting List

	Part	Dimensions	Qty.	Material
A	Floor joists, front/rear	1½ in. x 2½ in. x 72 in.	2	Pressure-treated ACQ
B	Floor joists	1½ in. x 2½ in. x 27 in.	4	Pressure-treated ACQ
C	Floor platform	¾ in. x 30 in. x 72 in.	1	Pressure-treated ACQ plywood
D	Left side studs	1½ in. x 2½ in. x 84½ in.	2	Douglas fir
E	Right side studs	1½ in. x 2½ in. x 90½ in.	2	Douglas fir
F	Front/rear wall studs	1½ in. x 3½ in. x 87½ in.	4	Douglas fir
G	Top front/rear studs	1½ in. x 2½ in. x 69 in.	2	Douglas fir
H	Top end studs	1½ in. x 2½ in. x 25 in.	2	Douglas fir
I	Top mid studs	1½ in. x 2½ in. x 27 in.	2	Douglas fir
J	Door top plate	1½ in. x 2½ in. x 24 in.	1	Pressure-treated ACQ
K	Roof top	¾ in. x 30 in. x 72 in.	1	Pressure-treated ACQ plywood
L	Nail board	1½ in. x 3½ in. x 69 in.	1	Douglas fir
M	Side and rear siding	⅝ in. x 4 ft. x 8 ft.	2	Exterior T-111 siding
N	End siding	¾ in. x 5½ in. x 40 in.	~17 pieces	Cedar
O	Front siding	¾ in. x 5½ in. x 30 in.	~50 pieces	Cedar

Tool and Garden Shed cont'd

Part		Dimensions	Qty.	Material
P	Door trim	½ in. x 1½ in. x 14'	1	Cedar
Q	Doorframe	1½ in. x 2½ in. x 79¾ in.	2	Douglas fir
R	Doorframe	1½ in. x 2½ in. x 20¾ in.	2	Douglas fir

Note: Measurements reflect the actual thickness of dimension lumber.

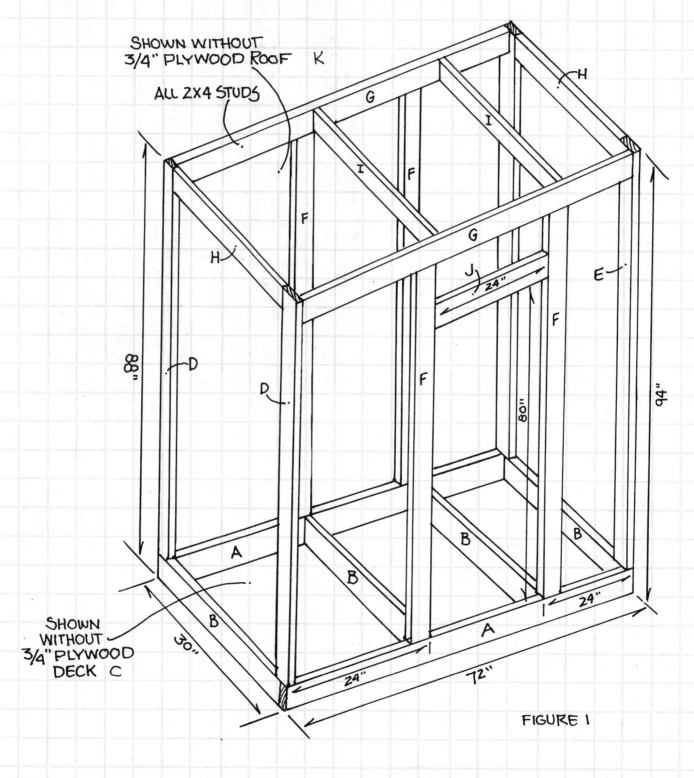

SHOWN WITHOUT 3/4" PLYWOOD ROOF   K

ALL 2X4 STUDS

SHOWN WITHOUT 3/4" PLYWOOD DECK C

FIGURE 1

Building the Tool and Garden Shed

Construct the floor platform

1. Cut the floor joists and floor platform (A, B, and C) to the sizes shown in the cutting list.
2. Set the front and rear floor joists (A) on edge on a flat work surface, approximately 30 inches apart. Measure and use a square to make marks at 24-inch centers along the faces of both joists. Refer to the bottom of figure 1.
3. Position four of the floor joists (B) so that one is located on each end and the other two are equally spaced between them. Nail the joists together using two 16d nails.
4. Place the floor platform (C) on top of the bottom floor frame, aligning the outside edges of the platform with the outside edges of the joists. Nail the plywood to the joist using 8d nails.
5. Place the completed platform in the desired location. Set it down evenly on the ground with a cinder block under each corner. Use a level to ensure that the bottom platform is level.

Construct the side, rear, and front walls

1. Measure and cut pieces (D, E, F, G, H, I, J, and K) to the sizes shown in the cutting list.
2. Lay out the two left side studs (D) on edge. Place the top end stud (H) in between the top of the side studs and secure and toenail it in place with 8d nails.
3. Repeat step 2 for the two right side studs (E and H).
4. Place the left side wall upright on top of the bottom platform edge. Then nail through the bottom of the wall into the plywood floor using 10d nails. Repeat this process to raise the right side wall.
5. Place the top front stud (G) between the left and right walls. You'll need to enlist an extra set of hands to hold one end in place as you nail the other. Use two 16d nails and nail through the side stud and into the end of the top stud. Repeat the same for the top rear stud (G).

6. Referring to figure 1, measure and mark the locations for the front and rear wall studs (F) along the bottom and the top studs. Place the front and rear wall studs in place and mark the angled cut along the top stud. Then cut the studs to the desired length and toenail them in place using two 10d nails in each stud end.
7. Place the door top plate (J) in position as shown in figure 1 and toenail it in place using 8d nails in each end.
8. Place the top middle studs (I) in position and nail them in place using two 16d nails in each end.

Secure the roofing and siding

1. Place the roof top (K) in place on top of the top studs and nail it into place using 6d nails driven into the top studs. Before nailing, make sure that the plywood is flush with the outside edges of the ends and sides. Nails should be placed approximately every 8 inches along the studs.
2. Measure and cut the sideing panels (M) to fit the rear wall and the right-side end wall. Nail the panel along the studs using 1½-inch siding nails placed on 12-inch centers.
3. The shed shown here uses 1x6 tongue-and-groove cedar siding run diagonally across the front and left side, which are most visible. If you prefer, T-111 siding can be used to save on cost and ease of construction. To install the tongue-and-groove cedar siding, start by cutting one end of a piece of siding (N) at a 45-degree angle using a miter saw or circular saw.
4. Place the angled end of the siding in position on the left-side end wall and then mark out the necessary length and make the cut on a 45-degree angle. Nail the cedar siding in place using 1½-inch finish nails. Repeat this process for the remaining pieces along the side.
5. Repeat this same procedure for the front of the shed. You'll have to work a little slower because you have to cut around the opening for the door.

Tool and Garden Shed cont'd

6. Measure three pieces of trim (P) and nail them in place around the doorframe opening using 1½-inch finish nails.

Make and install the door

1. Assemble the doorframe using (Q) and (R). Toe-nail the corners together using 8d nails, and use a T-square to make sure the corners are square.
2. Place the doorframe on a flat surface. To cover the doorframe with cedar siding, following the same procedure you used to make the walls, cutting the siding at 45-degree angles as you work. Nail the pieces to the doorframe using 1½-inch finish nails.
3. Mount the door to the frame using two 4-inch hinges. Follow the manufacturer's instructions for installing the hinges. You can place the hinges on either side of the door, depending on what direction you want it to swing.
4. Install a doorknob following the manufacturer's instructions.

Install inside nail board

1. Mount the nail board (L) approximately 6 inches down from the top of the rear wall inside the shed.
2. Depending on the type of tools to be stored and hung, use either nails or hooks along the nail board.

Apply the finishing touches

1. Although it's not necessary, you may want to stain or paint the interior surfaces. If so, use an exterior-grade latex finish.
2. The roof should be stained or painted with an exterior-grade stain or paint. For a longer-lasting roof, install asphalt roll roofing.
3. Stain or paint the exterior walls using a finish rated for exterior use.

Workbench

Oh boy, do I love this project! All I can say is that if you intend to build any of the other projects in this book, or if you want a terrific gunsmith bench, or you need a place to work on your bow, arrows, broadheads, and other archery equipment, build this workbench as soon as you can.

A good, solid workbench is one of the first "tools" you will need. Although it's not the fanciest of workstations, believe me when I say it will serve you well no matter what you use it for—woodworking, archery, gunsmithing, or even fly tying! This project is easy to build and calls for using a relatively inexpensive lumber like Douglas fir. It's also solid enough to tackle the jobs that more elaborate and expensive workbenches are known for. The bench seen here has a vise for gunsmithing; if you build it for woodworking, then you will probably prefer a woodworking vise instead. If you're like us, you'll build a few of these workbenches—one for every type of work you do.

The drawings show typical dimensions for a workbench, but it's easy to adjust the size of the bench to better match your body height, available wall space, and whatever vise you plan to install. You can also include a pegboard behind the bench, which comes in handy for hanging tools. If you do decide to add a pegboard, be sure to use a heavy $1/4$-inch board—it's both easier to install and less likely to give when you hang or remove tools.

If you are like most people, you build projects on the floor of the basement, garage, or wherever you can find a little open space. Like mine, your knees take a real beating working this way. Also, it's not the most efficient way to build things.

After building this bench and installing a vise, you can bang away on any project to your heart's content. This bench is so easy to construct and install that I have two in my home basement, one in my garden shed, two in the barn at my farm, and one in the basement of my farmhouse. Each serves a different function: woodworking, archery, gunsmithing, fly tying, general tool storage, and so on. And I'm thinking of building a couple more! Adding this workbench to the top of your things-to-build list will prove to be a terrific decision. So what are you waiting for? Get started building a couple right now.

Workbench

Overall Size: 70 in. long, 28 in. wide, 40 in. high

Tools Needed

- Circular saw, table saw, or handsaw
- Tape measure
- Chisel
- T-square or combination square
- Hammer

Materials

- Common nails—sizes 10d, 8d, and 6d
- Wood glue

Cutting List

	Part	Dimensions	Qty.	Material
A	Front legs	$1\frac{1}{2}$ in. x $5\frac{1}{2}$ in. x 38 in.	2	Douglas fir
B	Rear legs and rear support	$1\frac{1}{2}$ in. x $5\frac{1}{2}$ in. x 76 in.	2	Douglas fir
C	Front/rear leg supports	$1\frac{1}{2}$ in. x $5\frac{1}{2}$ in. x 43 in.	4	Douglas fir
D	Side leg supports	$1\frac{1}{2}$ in. x $5\frac{1}{2}$ in. x $27\frac{1}{2}$ in.	4	Douglas fir
E	Bench top	$1\frac{1}{2}$ in. x $5\frac{1}{2}$ in. x 70 in.	5	Douglas fir
F	Bench top back	$1\frac{1}{2}$ in. x $5\frac{1}{2}$ in. x 70 in.	1	Douglas fir
G	Bottom shelf	$1\frac{1}{2}$ in. x $5\frac{1}{2}$ in. x 46 in.	4	Douglas fir
H	Bench top braces	$\frac{3}{4}$ in. x $1\frac{1}{2}$ in. x $27\frac{1}{2}$ in.	2	Douglas fir
I	Top pegboard	$\frac{1}{4}$ in. x 32 in. x 46 in.	1	Masonite

Note: Measurements reflect the actual thickness of dimension lumber.

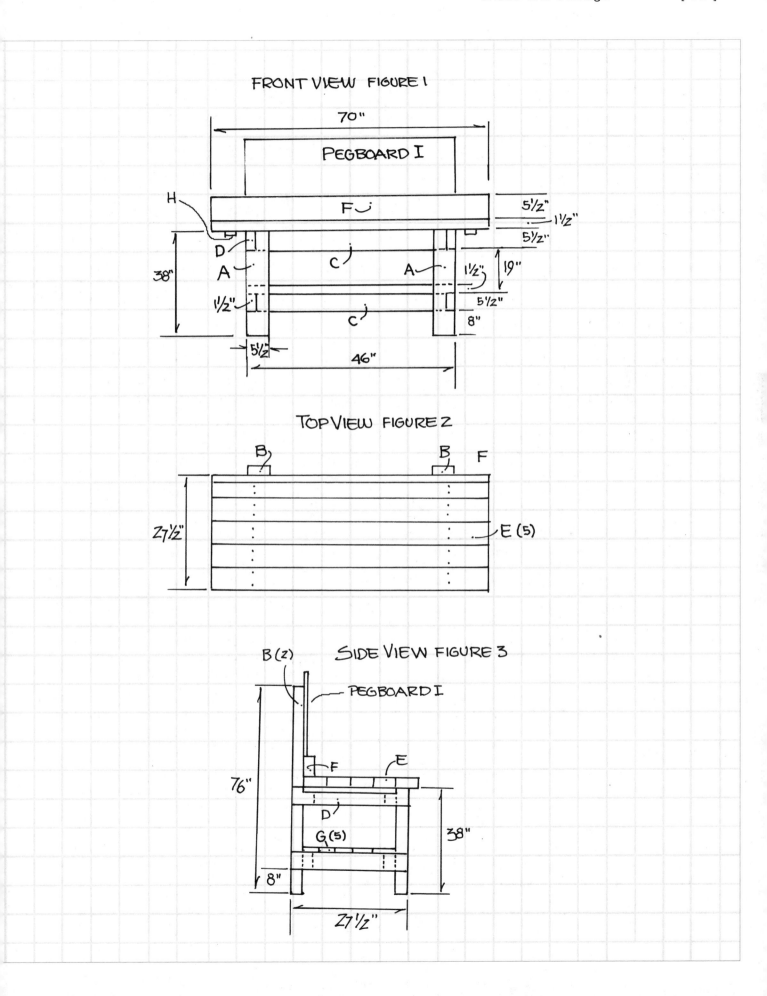

FRONT VIEW FIGURE 1

70"

PEGBOARD I

H
F
5½"
1½"
5½"
D
A
C
A
1½"
19"
38"
C
5½"
1½"
8"
5½"
46"

TOP VIEW FIGURE 2

B
B
F
27½"
E (5)

SIDE VIEW FIGURE 3

B (2)
PEGBOARD I
F
E
76"
D
G (5)
38"
8"
27½"

Workbench cont'd

Building the Workbench

Construct the bench base

1. Cut the legs and supports (A, B, C, and D) to the lengths shown in the cutting list using a circular saw or handsaw.
2. Notch out the mortises on the front legs (A) and rear legs (B) as follows: from the bottom of the legs measure 8 inches and 5½ inches up, then square off the marks 1½ inches deep. Measure up from that point to 19 inches and 24½ inches, then square off the marks 1½ inches deep. Using a table saw, circular saw, or handsaw, make 1½-inch deep cuts into the legs at the marks. You can take multiple passes between the two marks, then use a chisel to notch out the 5½-inch mortises. Refer to the front view, figure 1.
3. Lay out one of the front legs (A) and one of the rear legs (B) approximately 28 inches apart on a flat surface. Place the two side leg supports (D) in the notched mortises on the legs. Make sure that the ends of the side supports are flush with the fronts and backs of the legs. Using wood glue and three 10d nails at each joint, nail the side leg supports into the legs. Use a T-square to ensure that all joints are square prior to nailing.
4. Repeat step 3 to assemble the other side.
5. Set each of the side leg structures (from steps 3 and 4) upright and approximately 46 inches apart. Place two of the front and rear leg supports (C) in the front notches. Make sure that the ends are snug against the side leg supports and then glue and nail them in place using wood glue and 8d nails.
6. Use two 10d nails and nail through the side supports into the ends of the front leg supports at all four corners.
7. Repeat step 5 to construct the back of the bench.

Build the bench top and shelf

1. Measure and cut the bench top (E), bench top back (F), bottom shelf (G), and bench top braces (H) to the sizes shown in the cutting list.
2. Place the five bench top pieces (E) on top of the bench base, positioning them so that the bench top overhangs evenly on both ends by approximately 12 inches. Using wood glue and 10d nails, secure the bench top in place by nailing through it and into the top of the side leg supports (D). Use two nails on both ends of each board and make sure that the bench top pieces are snug to each other.
3. Place the bench top back (F) on top of the bench top and flush to the rear leg supports. Use wood glue and 10d nails to secure it in place.
4. Position each of the bench top braces (H) underneath the bench top. Secure them in place using wood glue and 6d nails driven into the bench top. Position these braces evenly on both sides.
5. Place the bottom shelf pieces (G) on the lower side leg supports and space them evenly between the legs. Use wood glue and 10d nails driven into the side leg supports to secure them in place.

Secure the pegboard (optional)

1. Place the pegboard (I) in place on top of the bench top back (F). Nail the pegboard in place using 6d nails driven into the rear leg supports.
2. If you do not need a pegboard to hang your tools, simply cut the excess of the rear leg support even with the top of the bench top back using a handsaw.
3. The bench can be left freestanding or secured in place against a wall. If you're going to mount a vise on the bench, we highly recommend bolting the bench to a wall using two 4-inch x $\frac{3}{8}$-inch lag bolts with washers driven through the rear legs.

CHAPTER 6

Handy Outdoor Projects

- Garden Gate
- Shooting Table Rest and Bench
- Shooting Range Backstop

Garden Gate

Gates—especially locking gates—are like fences. They keep neighbors and critters outside of your property, garden, pool, or other restricted area. They say the best neighbor is only as good as your fence and its gate. Well, I agree. I have a few neighbors at my farm that I would like to not only gate off, but block their view with a 12-foot-high fence as well!

There are less aggravating and more practical uses for gates as well. They can be used to keep pets within an enclosure, to provide easy entry into a fenced garden, or to make an entryway look better and more inviting.

Leo built this particular gate as a pleasing way to enter into his pool area (he lives in South Hampton and has a beautiful bay as his backyard. Why he needs a pool is beyond me—but hey, I don't live in ritzy South Hampton, so what do I know). In any event, the gate made a terrific addition to the entryway of the pool.

According to Leo, "this handsome-looking gate will last many years and give you a pleasing look for any entryway. I used Filipino mahogany, but you can use cedar, oak, or just treated lumber if you want to save some money on the cost of wood. If you use treated lumber, you should plan on painting or staining it.

"After spending considerable time shopping at local fence and gate companies and searching on the Web, I found that the prices varied from at least $600 to well over $1000 for standard-size gates. I decided to make this custom gate. It cost less than $350 and I was able to custom-fit it to the exact size needed to replace an existing chain-link fence. It took approximately eight hours to make and install the gate over a two-day period. It can easily be modified to fit your project's specific needs."

Garden Gate

Tools Needed

- Table saw, radial-arm saw, or handsaw
- Jigsaw
- Screw gun
- Drill
- Belt sander or random-orbit sander
- Posthole digger
- Shovel
- Level

Materials

- Wood glue
- Wood screws, 2½-inch and 1½-inch
- Two 80-pound bags of concrete/gravel ready mix
- Tar or other sealant
- Four temporary cross supports, 1½" x 1½" x 5' long
- Latches
- Hinges
- Gate handle
- Finish material

Overall Size:
76 in. wide,
7 ft. 6 in. high

Cutting List

	Part	Dimensions	Qty.	Material
A	Gate post	3½ in. x 3½ in. x 10 ft.	2	Filipino mahogany
B	Top trellis cross braces	1 in. x 5½ in. x 76 in.	2	Filipino mahogany
C	Trellis brackets	1½ in. x 5½ in. x 24 in.	5	Filipino mahogany
D	Trellis laterals	1½ in. x 1½ in. x 6 ft.	7	Filipino mahogany
E	Gate frame verticals	1 in. x 3½ in. x 42 in.	2	Filipino mahogany
F	Gate frame horizontals	1 in. x 3½ in. x 40½ in.	2	Filipino mahogany
G	Gate posts	1 in. x 2½ in. x 54 in.	9	Filipino mahogany

Note: Measurements reflect the actual thickness of dimension lumber.

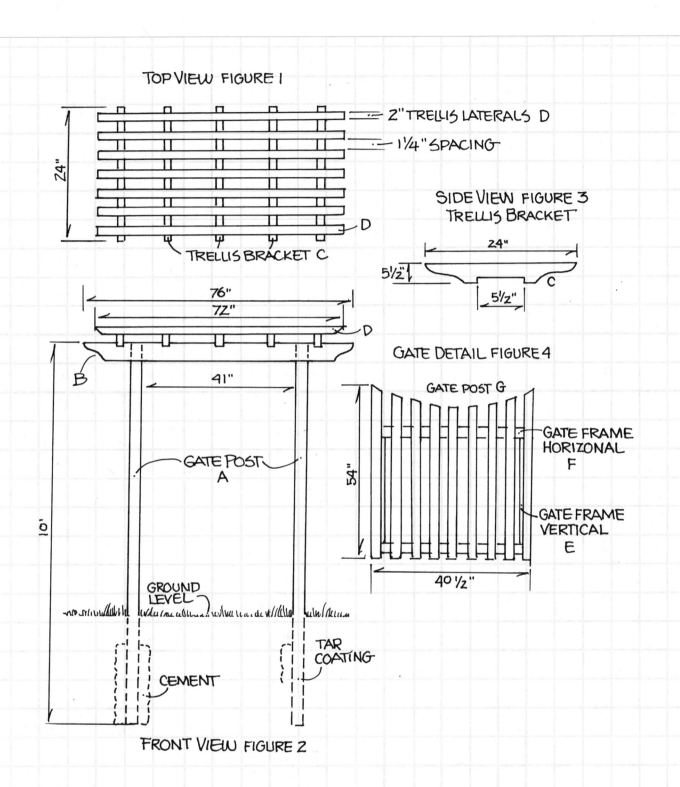

TOP VIEW FIGURE 1

2" TRELLIS LATERALS D

1¼" SPACING

SIDE VIEW FIGURE 3
TRELLIS BRACKET

24"

5½"

5½"   C

D

TRELLIS BRACKET C

76"

72"

D

GATE DETAIL FIGURE 4

GATE POST G

41"

GATE FRAME
HORIZONAL
F

GATE POST
A

54"

GATE FRAME
VERTICAL
E

10'

GROUND
LEVEL

40½"

TAR
COATING

CEMENT

B

FRONT VIEW FIGURE 2

Building the Garden Gate

Assemble the side posts and the top trellis

1. Cut the top trellis cross braces (B) to overall
   size and shape. It is easiest to cut the profiles
   on the ends of the braces with a jigsaw.

2. Install a cross brace (B) on both sides of the
   two posts (A) so that there is a 14-inch overhang on each side. The inside dimensions between the posts should match your desired

Garden Gate cont'd

gate opening plus ½ inch. For this gate, the posts are 41 inches apart. Attach the braces to the posts using wood glue and three 2½-inch wood screws on each end. Repeat this same procedure on both sides of the posts.

3. Cut the size and shape of the five trellis brackets (C) as shown in figure 3. Mount the trellis brackets above the top trellis cross braces (B), as shown, using wood glue and 2½-inch wood screws.

4. Cut the size and shape of the trellis laterals (D). The ends should be cut to 45-degree angles. Evenly space the trellis laterals (D) on top of the five trellis brackets (C) and secure them using glue and 2½-inch screws.

Make the garden gate

1. Referring to figure 4, cut the gate posts (G) to length from standard 5/4 x 6-inch stock. After cutting them to length, rip them at the table saw so that each board gives you two posts that are just over 2½ inches wide.

2. On a clean, flat surface, lay out the rectangular gate frame using the two gate frame verticals (E) and the two gate frame horizontals (F) all cut to size.

3. Evenly space the gate posts (G) on top of the gate frame so that approximately 1 inch overhangs the bottom gate frame horizontal (F). Secure each gate post to the frame using glue and 1½-inch wood screws. Drive the screws through the gate frame and into the posts so that the screws are not visible on the front of the gate posts.

4. Mark an oval pattern on the top of the gate using a pencil attached to a string. Center the string above and off the gate posts but align it with the centerline of the gate. Hold one end of the string in that spot and swing the pencil at the other end to mark out the arch shape on the posts.

5. Cut the oval shape using a jigsaw. Smooth the cut ends of the gate posts using a belt sander or random-orbit sander.

Install the posts and trellis in the ground

1. Dig two holes, approximately 30 inches deep, using a posthole digger. Space the centers of the holes roughly 45 inches apart.

2. Coat the bottom 30 inches of each post with a tar sealant and allow it to dry thoroughly.

3. Place the posts in the holes and temporarily secure them in place using diagonal cross supports. Use a level to make sure that the top of the trellis is level. Check to see that the side posts are level also, and adjust the cross supports as needed. Use two 2 x 4's for your temporary cross supports for each post. They should be at least 5' long. Nail one end to the 4 x 4' post aproximately 3 feet from the bottom. Nail the other one on the opposite side of the post. Adjust the bottom of the supports in the dirt as you level the post. Repeat for the other post.

4. Mix up one bag of ready mix concrete/gravel and shovel it into each hole. Make sure you surround the posts on all sides and tamp the concrete down with the shovel as you work. After shoveling in the concrete, recheck to make sure everything is still level and make adjustments as necessary. Then allow the concrete to dry overnight.

5. The next morning, remove the temporary cross supports, backfill the hole with dirt, and level off the grade.

Attach the gate and hardware

1. Position the gate between the two posts, propping it up with a piece of wood and adjusting until you get the desired clearance off the ground.

2. Align the top and bottom hinges so that the longer leaves of the hinges line up with the gate frame horizontals. Drill ¹⁄₁₆-inch pilot holes and secure the hinges in place using wood screws.

3. Secure the gate latch on the top of the gate and install the handle midway down the outside of the gate.

4. Sand and finish the gate as you see fit.

Shooting Table Rest and Bench

After slowly stalking the big herd bull and his harem for two hours, we were beginning to think we would never find them. Our guide, Kevin, kept assuring me and my cameraman, Leo, that with a little more patience and work, the chances of catching up to the bull and his cows were better than fifty-fifty. Fair enough odds for me, so we continued our stalk.

Almost an hour later, we came to a knoll that looked down over an open grassy area along the edge of a woodlot that bordered a very steep ravine. Slowly we crawled up to the knoll's top and peeked over to see if the herd of elk was anywhere in sight. Unlike the dozen or so other knolls we had checked in vain, at this one we found our quarry.

Below us cows fed contently as we watched them unnoticed. It took only seconds to spot the huge herd bull as he lay in his bed surveying his harem. We pushed ourselves off the knoll and slightly back down its edge to discuss our next move.

"He didn't see or wind us," Kevin said. "Do you think you can make the shot?"

"I don't know," I said. "Let's put the Leica rangefinder on him and find out exactly how far away he is. Then I'll know."

"That means climbing over the hill again, which increases our chances of being seen. Wait here and let me go alone," Kevin replied.

Moments later, he back-crawled to me and said the bull was 255 yards from the top of the knoll. "Can you make a shot that long accurately?"

"Is he still lying in his bed?" I asked.

"Yes," Kevin whispered.

Well, even though it is the ultimate achievement to stalk up to a big-game animal in his bed, the animal's position limits the amount of body visible to hit cleanly. "Let's give it a try. If I see a clean shot opportunity, I'll take it."

Within minutes, the three of us quietly pushed our flattened bodies over the top of the small hill. The tension built as Leo set the camera up and I waited for the go-ahead to shoot. I always have to wait to hear from the cameraman before taking an animal.

"Take him anytime you're ready," Leo whispered.

I placed the scope's crosshairs on the bull's neck and squeezed. The sound of the shot surprised me even though I was expecting it. The bull fell over without ever knowing what had happened. In reaction to the report of the rifle, his cows raced off in every direction. One clean shot from my Ruger .30-06 loaded with Winchester 180-grain Fail Safe bullets dropped the bull before he had a chance to notice or wind our presence.

Making a shot like this is always challenging, and you should never take a chance on making a clean shot at a bedded-down animal unless you are positive you can end the hunt without incident. That takes practice, confidence in your firearm, and range time.

Even though I had already spent hours sighting in my rifle at the range on my farm (see page 84 for more on building your own range) prior to this hunt, I'd always had to take the time to sight in again once I arrived at camp—just to be sure my gun wasn't jarred off zero on the plane or while driving over the rough roads on the way to a ranch.

The time spent making sure your gun is zeroed in builds your confidence when you have to make a shot. In this case, the distance was longer than I usually like to shoot, but not out of the range of my comfort zone. The knowledge that my firearm was shooting accurately allowed me to make the decision to take a once-in-a-lifetime trophy bull elk at 255 yards. The bull was a 7x8 whose antlers scored 375 B&C! He was the biggest bull elk I have ever taken. I shot him on the Cree Indian Reservation at Cree River Outfitters in Saskatchewan in November 2005.

To end any hunt successfully, your shot has to be on target. The more range time you put in to achieve better shooting habits and confidence, the more you increase your odds of hitting what you're aiming at each and every time. Although every hunter wounds an animal or two during his or her hunting career, time spent practicing at the range minimizes these unwelcome moments afield.

This project complements the outdoor shooting range also found in this book. As part of that project we realized that we also needed to include a shooting bench and seat to go along with the range backstop. We wanted it not only to be sturdy, but also something that would provide maximum comfort when sighting in firearms from inside an enclosed range house or when sitting outside. It also needed to be small enough to be easily transportable. We had seen similar projects at local shooting ranges, and after making a few modifications and improvements, we came up with this design.

We have used it outdoors and from our shooting shed. If you intend to keep it solely outdoors, you should use only ACQ-treated lumber. Although treated lumber is more expensive than Douglas fir, it will withstand the weather better and last much longer. Fortunately, we had leftover lumber from a recently completed deck, so this project didn't cost much to build. If you'll be shooting from a shooting shed or other enclosure, there is no need to spend the extra money on treated lumber. You could also use cedar, which would be a bit lighter than ACQ. However, we like a heavier bench—even though it is more cumbersome to move around, the weight prevents the bench from moving or jumping after each shot. This is especially important when sighting in big-bore firearms. A heavy, sturdy bench will provide you with more accurate shooting results every time.

If you plan on leaving the table rest and bench in a permanent location, make the legs about 18 inches longer, and then bury a portion of the legs to provide more stability. The buried portion of the legs should be treated with asphalt or an exterior-grade oil-based paint.

Shooting Table Rest and Bench

Overall Size: 48 in. long, 36 in. wide, 33 in. high

Tools Needed

- Table saw, circular saw, or handsaw
- Jigsaw
- Screw gun or drill and driver set
- Compound miter saw or hand miter box
- Belt sander, random-orbit sander, or sandpaper

Materials

- Exterior wood glue
- Exterior wood screws: sizes 2¼-inch, 1¾-inch 1½-inch
- Exterior-grade stain or preservative

Cutting List

Shooting Table

	Part	Dimensions	Qty.	Material
A	Table legs	3½ in. x 3½ in. x 32 in.	4	Pressure-treated ACQ
B	Table top/mid side rails	1 in. x 3½ in. x 32 in.	4	Pressure-treated ACQ
C	Table rear rails	1 in. x 3½ in. x 46 in.	2	Pressure-treated ACQ
D	Table front rails	1 in. x 3½ in. x 5½ in.	2	Pressure-treated ACQ
E	Table mid-support	1½ in. x 3½ in. x 44 in.	1	Pressure-treated ACQ
F	Table angle support	1 in. x 3½ in. x 9½ in.	2	Pressure-treated ACQ
G	Table top	¾ in. x 36 in. x 48 in.	1	Pressure-treated ACQ plywood
H	Table side braces	1 in. x 3½ in. x 14 in.	2	Pressure-treated ACQ

Shooting Table Rest and Bench cont'd

Bench

Part		Dimensions	Qty.	Material
I	Bench legs	1½ in. x 2½ in. x 17 in.	4	Pressure-treated ACQ
J	Bench front/rear rails	1 in. x 2½ in. x 14 in.	4	Pressure-treated ACQ
K	Bench side rails	1 in. x 2½ in. x 12 in.	4	Pressure-treated ACQ
L	Bench top	¾ in. x 16 in. x 16 in.	1	Pressure-treated ACQ plywood

Note: Measurements reflect the actual thickness of dimension lumber.

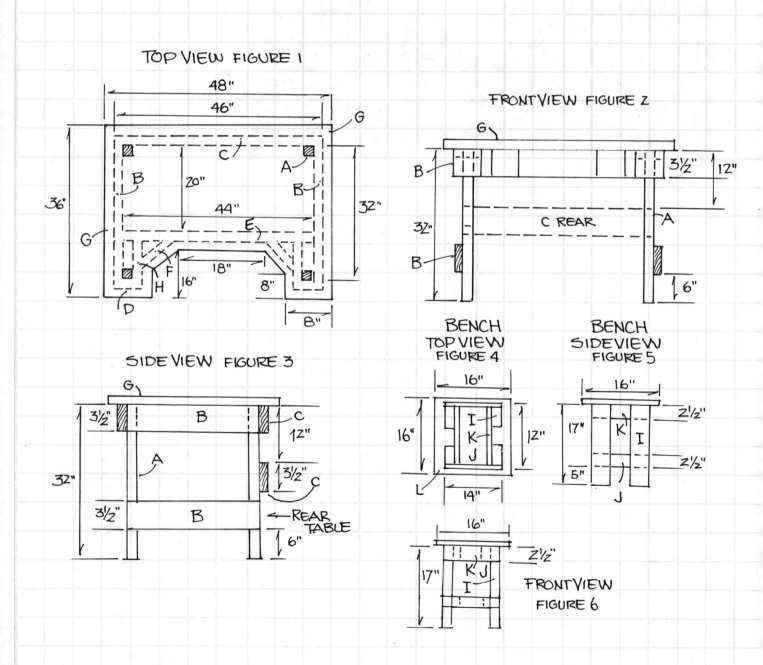

Building the Shooting Table Rest and Bench

Construct the shooting table rest

1. Measure and cut all the parts for the table rest (A, B, C, D, E, F, G, and H) to the sizes shown in the cutting list. You can make the bulk of these cuts using a table saw, circular saw, or handsaw, but you'll need a jigsaw to cut the table top (G) to shape.

2. Lay out two of the table legs (A) on a flat surface approximately 32 inches apart. Secure two of the table top/mid side rails (B) in place using wood glue and two $2\frac{1}{4}$-inch wood screws (refer to figures 1 and 3). Repeat this step for the other two table legs and another top/middle side rail.

3. Stand the two sets of table legs upright with the fronts of the legs on a flat surface, spaced approximately 46 inches apart. Secure the table rear rails (C) to the rear of the leg sets using glue and two $2\frac{1}{4}$-inch wood screws. One rail should be at the top and the other in the middle position, as shown in the top view and the side view (figures 1 and 3).

4. Turn over the entire leg assembly and lay the back a flat surface. Secure the table mid-support (E) in between both of the tabletop side rails, as shown in top view (figure 1), using wood glue and two $2\frac{1}{4}$-inch wood screws. Make sure that the table mid-support is flush with the tabletop side rails.

5. Secure the table side braces (H) in place using wood glue and two $2\frac{1}{4}$-inch screws, making sure that they are flush with the top rails. Also, install two screws from the table mid-support into the ends of the table side braces.

6. Secure the table front rails (D) in place using wood glue and two $2\frac{1}{4}$-inch screws.

7. Cut the ends of each of the table angle supports (F) at 45-degree angles using a compound miter saw or a handsaw and miter box. Secure them in place using glue and two $1\frac{3}{4}$-inch wood screws at each location.

8. Stand the table support structure upright on the four legs. Lay the table top (G) on top of the table support structure. Position it so that it overhangs approximately 1 inch on the sides, front, and rear. Secure the table top (G) using wood glue and $1\frac{1}{2}$-inch wood screws driven in around the edges.

9. Using a jigsaw, cut out the front gap of the table top to the dimensions as shown in figure 1.

Construct the bench

1. Measure and cut all of the bench parts (I, J, K, and L) to the sizes shown in the cutting list.

2. Lay out two of the bench legs (I) on a flat surface approximately 12 inches apart. Secure the bench side rails (K) to the insides of the legs using wood glue and two $1\frac{3}{4}$-inch wood screws at each location. (Refer to the top view and side view, figures 4 and 6.) Repeat this same procedure for the other two bench legs.

3. Lay out the two sets of bench legs approximately 14 inches apart. Secure the bench front rails (J) to the legs using wood glue and two $1\frac{3}{4}$-inch wood screws at each location. Repeat this process on the other set of bench legs.

4. Stand the bench leg structure upright. Lay the bench top (L) on top of the bench structure and position it so that it overhangs the legs approximately 1 inch on each side. Secure it in place using wood glue and $1\frac{1}{2}$-inch wood screws driven in around the edges.

Apply the finishing touches

1. Scrape off any excess glue and smooth any rough surfaces or edges using a belt sander or random-orbit sander, or by hand.

2. Since we used exterior wood on our project, it was not necessary to apply a finish. However, if you plan on leaving it outdoors, we recommend an exterior-grade wood stain or preservative.

Shooting Range Backstop

As any firearm hunter knows, having your own shooting range is not only convenient; it also helps make you a better hunter, too. Why? Well, the convenience of having your own shooting range enables you become more comfortable with your firearms, practice more, and build strong shooting skills. Most importantly, having your own range helps make you a more confident shooter. And confidence makes you a more accurate shooter.

Almost all hunters use scopes these days, so after you have mounted your scope or had it mounted at the local gun shop, be sure to have it bore-sighted at 100 yards. Once this is done, the next step is to begin sight-in at 25 yards. Use targets that have blaze-orange or yellow-and-black high-visibility bull's-eyes, like the Shoot-N-C Targets™. Also, to prevent your muscles from becoming cramped or tense, make sure you have a comfortable and sturdy shooting bench to shoot from (see our Shooting Table Rest and Bench on page 79).

Next, rest the forearm of your firearm in a secure shooting vise like the Lead Sled PFT™, the Rock BR1000™, the Rest™, the Ransom Rifle Master™, or some other type of sturdy and reliable shooting rest. If you don't have a commercial-type shooting rest, you can use a couple of 8- to 10-pound sandbags.

Remember, never rest any part of a rifle, particularly the barrel, on a hard surface. This will cause the rifle to kick away from the hard surface when you shoot, giving you a false point of impact. If you are using a variable power scope, set it to the power that provides the sharpest sight picture. Many scopes provide sharper images set slightly below their maximum magnification. For example, the view through a 4–12x scope may look better at 10x or 11x than it does at 12x.

After loading a round into the chamber, put the crosshairs directly on the center of the bull's-eye. And try to learn to shoot with both eyes open—by closing one eye you eliminate half your view. Fire one round. Even though you bore-sighted your rifle, the bullet hole is probably not going to be in the center of the target at 25 yards, but it should be somewhere on the paper. Shoot a couple of times to make sure you have a tight grouping.

If your rifle is now hitting within an inch or less of the point of aim at 25 yards, it should be on paper at 100 yards. Let your barrel cool for a while, and then shoot at your 100-yard target. I like to use Outers "Score Keeper" target. It has a central bull's-eye and four smaller bull's-eyes, one in each corner. It is also overlaid with 1-inch grid lines, making it easy to see how far your bullet holes are from the point of aim using only your spotting scope.

Fire three shots at the bull's-eye at 100 yards. For many typical long-range rifle calibers, such as the .243 Winchester, .270 Winchester with 130–140 grain bullets, .280 Winchester, 7mm Magnum with 140–160 grain bullets, .300 Magnum with

Designed with a platform large and sturdy enough for two hunters, the Buddy Sidekick Stand is the one to build when you're teaching a new or young hunter and need to take him or her into the stand with you.

The nine-gun rack can easily be a six- or twelve-gun rack, depending upon your needs, but in any size, it provides a safe, convenient place to temporarily set your firearms while taking a break from the hunt.

Anyone who has ever tried to balance on one foot while putting on his boots or fussed with bib coveralls and other tricky outdoors clothing will appreciate having a spot in the mud room, garage, or cabin to sit down and get ready in comfort.

This bluebird house adheres to all the specifications required by the North American Bluebird Society for creating a proper home for this species. It's a great project for a young woodworker—with dad's supervision.

Everyone needs a shed, and this one is very easy to construct off the side of a garage or home. It will make a huge difference in your ability to organize lawn and garden tools, fertilizer, mulch, and lots more.

A custom-made gate adds a touch of class to the patio, pool, or garden and can keep out unwanted critters.

Time on the range increases hunting success, so time spent at the shooting bench should be hassle-free. This shooting rest and bench are easy to transport and are designed so the shooter is comfortable and able to focus on the crosshairs.

An easy stand to build, the Gotcha Tree Stand's major requirement is two healthy trees appropriately spaced. Choosing larger trees minimizes sway in the wind.

The Stump-Sitter Tree Stand can be permanently mounted to a tree, if necessary, but you can also easily remove the mounting bolts to transport it to a new hunting spot.

You'll need to find a triple-trunk tree or a tight cluster of three individual trees in which to build the Master Hunter Stand, but its configuration allows for a very stable and roomy platform with the option of a shed roof.

The Master Hunter Stand platform is large enough for two fixed seats, allowing for varying shooting angles, but a hunter could also easily use a moveable seat. Add camouflage wrap around the stand frame for greater concealment.

Built with treated lumber, the Master Hunter Stand, like the others in this book, is designed to last many seasons. Camouflaging the underside of both the platform and shed roof is a good idea.

165–180 grain bullets, or .338 Magnum with a 200 grain bullet, the rifle should be sighted to hit a point of impact at approximately 2½ inches above the point of aim at 100 yards.

In other words, aim exactly at the center of the bull's-eye and your bullets should hit the target about 2½ inches above the center of the bull's-eye. That maximizes the point-blank range of your rifle, eliminating the need to hold over any big-game animal from the muzzle out to a distance of about 300 yards (or more) with the cartridges and loads mentioned above. However, it is wise to check the Rifle Trajectory Table for any caliber you are shooting to be sure of the 100-yard point of impact and maximum point-blank range (MPBR) for your cartridge and load.

If you are sighting in a medium-range rifle like a .30-30 with 150–170 grain bullets, .300 Savage with 165–180 grain bullets, .30-06 with a 220 grain bullet, .32 Winchester Special with a 170 grain bullet, .338-57 O'Connor with 200–225 grain bullets, .35 Remington with a 200 grain bullet, .358 Winchester with a 200 grain bullet, .416 Rigby with a 400 grain bullet, .444 Marlin with 240–300 grain bullets, or .450 Marlin with a 350 grain bullet, you will want your bullets to hit about 3 inches high with a center hold at 100 yards. This will give you an MPBR of about 200 to 250 yards, depending on the individual caliber and load. Once again, aim at the center of the bull's-eye, and adjust the actual point of the bullet's impact to be about 3 inches directly above your point of aim.

Once you have got your gun sighted in, it's advisable to shoot another three-shot group. Again, before each shot make sure that the barrel has time to cool. This step will provide the most accuracy.

Once the elevation is correct and the center of your group is the necessary 2½ inches above the point of aim, you can concentrate on bringing the windage adjustment into play—it only takes a few shots to determine whether you need to bring your shots to the left or right to hit the center of the bull's-eye. Nothing beats the enjoyment of knowing that you have done what it takes to make your firearm as accurate as it can be for your hunt.

We decided to build our shooting backstop and range primarily for guests at our farm. All hunters who are invited to hunt with us must sight in their firearms before they hunt. We accept no excuses about this rule. To drastically reduce the chances of wounding a buck or doe, it is important for our guests, as well as for us, to accept the responsibility of making sure firearms are zeroed in.

But what we have learned is that a good shooting range also provides countless hours of fun. Whether we are sighting in for our next hunt or just plinking at targets with the kids, we always enjoy our time at the range. Build your own range and you will quickly find out how much it will bring family and friends together to enjoy a day of shooting. This wall can be made wider or higher to meet your needs or desire. Simply follow the pattern of the anchor posts.

Shooting Range Backstop

Overall Size: 8 ft. long, 7 ft. to 8 ft. high, 12 in. deep

Tools Needed

- Backhoe
- Shovel
- Chain saw
- Level
- Drill and ½-inch drill bit
- Sledgehammer
- Tamper
- Rake

Materials

- Eight pieces of ½-inch rebar, 3 feet to 4 feet long
- Railroad nail spikes (for 12-inch x 12-inch posts, use spikes at least 16 inches long)
- Six to eight 40-pound bags of gravel or stone
- exterior oil, paint, or stain

Cutting List

	Part	Dimensions	Qty.	Material
A	Posts	12 in. x 12 in. x 8 ft. long	5	Exterior-lumber posts
B	Posts	12 in. x 12 in. x 3½ ft. long	2	Exterior-lumber posts
C	Posts	12 in. x 12 in. x 2 ft. long	3	Exterior-lumber posts
D	Posts	12 in. x 12 in. x 7 ft. long	1	Exterior-lumber post
E	Anchor posts	12 in. x 12 in. x 4 ft. long	3	Exterior-lumber posts
F	Top anchor post	12 in. x 12 in. x 5 ft. long	2	Exterior-lumber posts
G	Plywood	4 ft. x 8 ft.	2	Exterior plywood

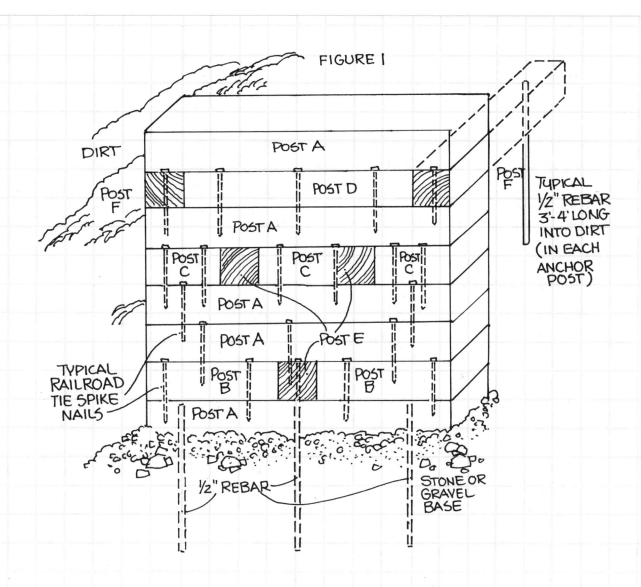

FIGURE 1

DIRT

POST A

POST F

POST D

POST A

POST C   POST C   POST C

POST A

POST A   POST E

TYPICAL RAILROAD TIE SPIKE NAILS

POST B   POST B

POST A

1/2" REBAR

STONE OR GRAVEL BASE

POST F

TYPICAL 1/2" REBAR 3'-4' LONG INTO DIRT (IN EACH ANCHOR POST)

Building a Shooting Range Backstop

Excavate the ground

1. Locate an area on your property where there is a naturally graded soil background to act as a backing to stop the path of your bullets.
2. Make sure that the embankment is not in the direction of any neighbors.
3. The finished backstop should be set at approximately 100 yards from where you intend to shoot. Measure this distance and mark it with temporary stakes in the ground. Most of my sighting is done between 50 and 100 yards. However, if you sight in at farther distances, then measure and mark accordingly.

4. Either by hand or using a small backhoe, dig out an appropriate amount of soil. The amount of dirt you remove depends upon the slope of the hill—clear an area at least 10 feet wide and 7 to 8 feet high. Clear away at least 4 feet behind the planned wall (you will fill this back in as the wall is competed). Square off the dirt in the back so it is perpendicular to the grade.

Assemble the back wall posts

1. Lay the first post (A) flat on the ground approximately 4 feet from the rear dirt wall and make sure it is level.

Shooting Range Backstop cont'd

2. Use a ½-inch drill bit to bore three holes evenly spaced along the 8-foot length through the ties and toward the grade. Use a sledgehammer to bang the rebar into the dirt so that it is flush to the top of the posts.

3. Lay one of the anchor posts (E) in the middle on top of the first post so that it is perpendicular to the wall. Backfill the first 12 inches of dirt behind the wall. As you backfill, tamp down the dirt with a tamper. Drive one of the long spike nails into the first post.

4. Predrill the hole in the end of the anchor post. Using a ½-inch drill bit, make a hole about 3 feet in from the front end of anchor post. Use the sledgehammer to bang the rebar into the dirt. Remember to tamp the dirt as you backfill behind the wall.

5. Lay two of the posts (B) on either side of the anchor post. Use two spike nails in each side to secure the posts to the lower level.

6. Lay the next post (A) on top of the second layer of posts. Use three spike nails to secure it to the lower beam. Predrill the holes in the upper post and repeat this process for the next layer of posts.

7. Lay two of the anchor posts (E) on top of next layer, spaced 2 feet from each end. Backfill the dirt behind the wall up to this level. Use the long spike nails to secure the anchor posts to the lower post on each side. Predrill the holes in the ends of the anchor posts about 3 feet in from the front end and use a sledgehammer to drive the rebar into the dirt. Remember to tamp the dirt as you backfill behind the wall.

8. Lay the posts (C) in between these two anchor posts. Use two spike nails to secure them to the lower post.

9. Lay the next posts (A) on top of the fifth layer of posts. Predrill the holes in the upper post

and use three spike nails to secure it to the lower beam.

10. Lay the post (D) on the next level, leaving a 1-foot space at each end. Use three spike nails to secure it to the lower beam.

11. Lay two of the anchor posts (F) on top of next layer at each end. Backfill the dirt behind the wall up to this level. Drive the long spikes nail into the lower post on each side. Predrill the holes in the ends of the anchor posts, about 4 feet from the front end of each. Use the sledgehammer to drive the rebar into the dirt. Remember to tamp down the dirt as you backfill behind the wall.

12. Lay the last post (A) on top. After predrilling, use three spike nails to secure it to the lower beam.

13. Nail plywood over the post to provide extra support and strength to the backdrop. This will also help absorb the bullets and extend the life of the post.

Finish backfilling and prepare the front ground

1. Finish backfilling the dirt behind the wall. Mound the dirt slightly higher than the top of the wall.

2. Coat the plywood with an exterior oil, paint, or stain to preserve the wood.

3. Empty the bags of stone or gravel in front of the wall and then even them out with a garden rake.

4. As you use the target and break down the plywood, replace or simply add layers of plywood to the face of the post wall.

CHAPTER 7

Animal Houses and Feeders

- Bluebird House
- Bird Feeder
- Rabbit House
- Bat House

Bluebird House

If you enjoy watching bluebirds, you already know that bluebird lovers are serious about their favorite winged friends. Many folks who build bluebird houses enthusiastically take on the extra work of establishing a "bluebird trail," meaning that they mount several houses along a trail or path. This tactic allows for multiple habitats and numerous opportunities for observation and appreciation of one of the nation's most popular and handsome birds. Our bluebird house is second to none, in that Leo was sure to adhere to all the specifications required by the North American Bluebird Society.

For instance, both Eastern and Western bluebirds use a 1½-inch entrance hole and prefer their nests 3 to 6 feet above the ground. Mountain bluebirds also like a 1½-inch entrance hole, but prefer their nests 5 to 10 feet above the ground. If you're building a birdhouse for use in zones where either Eastern or Mountain bluebirds dwell, keep these height preferences in mind. Because bluebirds have quite specific nesting requirements, it is important to understand that the key to attracting bluebirds is placing properly constructed nest boxes in suitable habitats.

Bluebirds are insectivorous during the nesting season, feeding mainly on ground-dwelling insects. Ideal bluebird habitats are open and barren or short-cut and sparsely grassed areas so they can see their food, with a few trees nearby for perching. Pesticide- and herbicide-free cattle or horse pastures, cemeteries, acreages, abandoned orchards, hike-and-bike trails, prairie coulees, lightly traveled roadsides, abandoned railroad rights-of-way, golf courses, open areas in parks, the edges of meadows, clear-cuts adjacent to or within forested areas that have been recently burned, and sagebrush flats provide excellent bluebird habitat. Bluebirds will also nest on the fringes of towns and cities, especially if they were nesting in those areas prior to development. Poor bluebird habitat includes areas that they naturally shun (i.e., city centers, densely wooded areas, or intensively farmed areas where there is a lack of natural habitat), areas where they are in competition with house wrens or house sparrows, or locations where the boxes are at risk of predation.

With all this in mind, another good reason for building a bluebird house is to help the species survive the onslaught of developers who have reduced their populations. Luckily, a lot of bird lovers—especially bluebird fans—took a keen interest in providing more housing for bluebirds and began putting up bluebird houses to provide additional habitats for these icons of American bird-watchers.

One of the organizations most important to the survival of the bluebird is the North American Bluebird Society. The bluebirds' survival is dependent upon the continued effort of this international organization to support and maintain the integrity of their continent-wide network of birdhouses. Increasingly, other songbird species that need cavities to raise their young are dependent upon the work of the North American Bluebird Society.

If you build a bluebird house to the North American Bluebird Society's specifications, the presence of the birds themselves will prove thanks enough for your effort to conserve our songbirds. Without your hands-on effort, this movement toward conservation cannot succeed.

Bluebird House

Tools Needed

- Table saw or handsaw
- Drill
- Hole saw, 1½-inch diameter
- Screw gun or hammer
- Sander

Materials

- Exterior wood glue
- Galvanized finish nails (sizes 2d and 4d) or galvanized screws (1½-inch)
- Latex silicon caulking
- Polyurethane glue
- Finish material such as paint or stain
- Two ¼-inch U-bolts with nuts and washers (optional)

Overall Size: 6 in. wide, 26 in. high, 10¼ in. deep

Cutting List

	Part	Dimensions	Qty.	Material
A	Exterior roof	¾ in. x 11¼ in. x 14 in.	1	Cedar
B	Inside roof	¾ in. x 4½ in. x 9½ in.	1	Cedar
C	Floor	¾ in. x 4½ in. x 3 in.	1	Cedar
D	Front panel	¾ in. x 4½ in. x 12½ in.	1	Cedar
E	Back support	¾ in. x 4½ in. x 26 in.	1	Cedar
F	Sides	¾ in. x 10¼ in. x 18 in.	2	Cedar

Note: Measurements reflect the actual thickness of dimension lumber.

Building the Bluebird House

Cut the parts to size

1. Use either a table saw or handsaw to cut the project parts (A, B, C, D, and E) to the sizes provided in the cutting list. For pieces (B), (C), and (E) the ends must be cut at an angle of 65 degrees, as shown in figure 1.

2. Mark out both angles on the sides (F), as shown in the illustration, on standard 1x12 lumber. Cut the sides to shape using either a table saw or a handsaw.

3. Using a 1½-inch hole saw, and drill the entrance hole in the front piece (D). The hole should be

Bluebird House cont'd

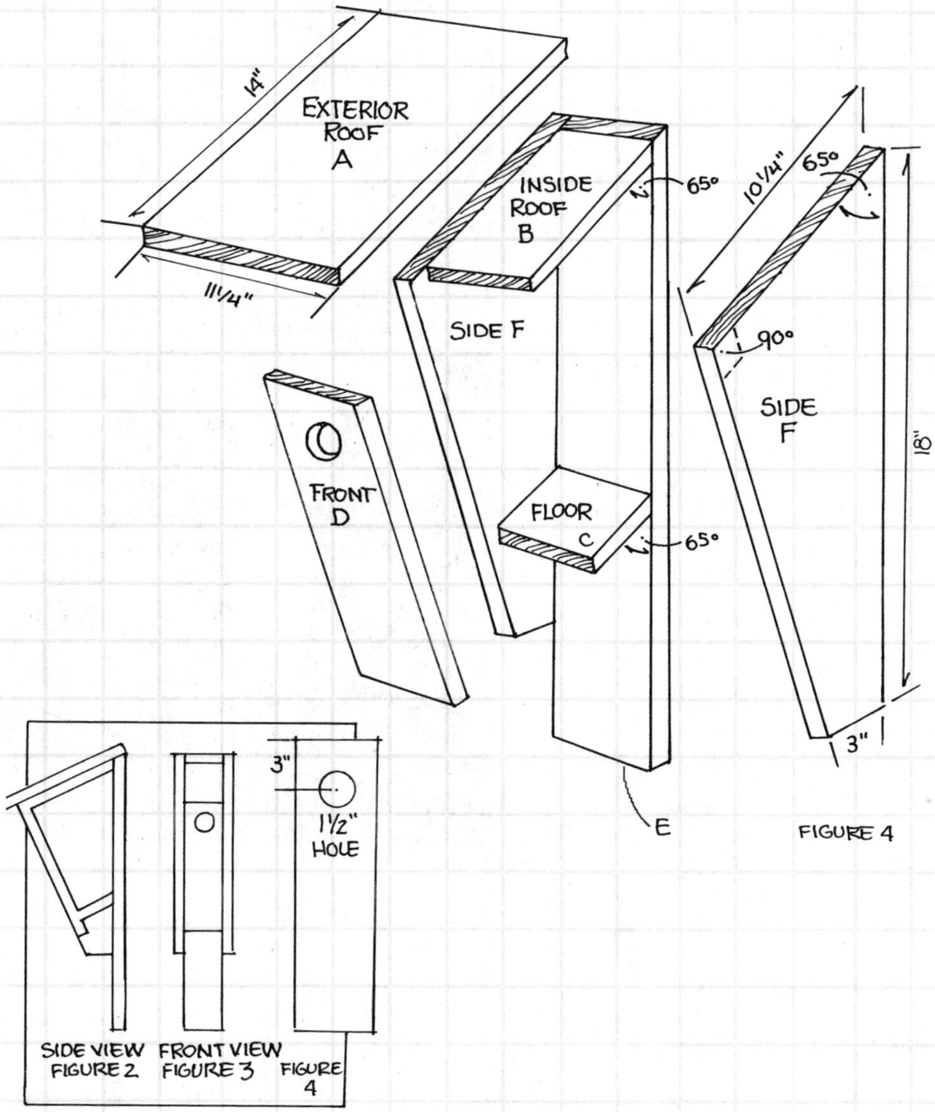

EXTERIOR ROOF A

14"

11¼"

INSIDE ROOF B

SIDE F

65°

10¼"

65°

90°

SIDE F

18"

FRONT D

FLOOR C

65°

3"

E

FIGURE 4

3"

1½" HOLE

3"

SIDE VIEW FIGURE 2

FRONT VIEW FIGURE 3

FIGURE 4

centered across the width of the board and 3 inches down from the top.

Assemble all the pieces

1. Attach the sides to the back plate using wood glue and either 1½-inch screws or 4d nails. The top ends of the sides should align with the top end of the back plate. Predrill all of your screw or nail holes to prevent the wood from splitting. (Note: To ease periodic clean-out of the bird house, don't apply glue to one of the side pieces and use wood screws to secure it. This

way, the side can be removed and reattached easily.)

2. Attach the inside roof to the sides and back plate using wood glue and screws or nails.

3. Glue and screw (or nail) the floor in place so that the square end is inset ¾ inch from the edge of the side pieces.

4. To seal the inside edges, caulk the interior seams with silicon.

5. Attach the front using wood glue and screws or nails. Screw from the sides and inside roof. Make sure that the entrance hole is on top.

6. Attach the exterior roof, making sure that it is flush with the back and evenly overhangs the sides.

Apply the finishing touches

1. Sand the entire surface using a sander.
2. Paint or stain the exterior surface if desired. Cedar will fare well in the weather even if you apply no finish.

3. Mount the Bluebird House in your desired location. You can mount it directly on a tree, on the side of a building, or atop a pole. To mount the birdhouse to a metal post or stake, use two $\frac{1}{4}$-inch U-bolts with nuts and washers.

Bird Feeder

One of the most popular woodworking projects for outdoor men and women is a bird feeder. You don't even have to be a bird-watcher to enjoy having a few bird feeders on your property. If you do enjoy spotting birds, however, then this project is sure to provide you with unlimited hours watching birds and other wildlife.

Bird feeders provide a source of food for a wide variety of wild birds, ranging from the tiny English sparrow to the beautiful robin, or even some of the larger species. By having a bird feeder in your yard, you'll guarantee yourself the chance to observe a wide variety of birds that stop by for a free lunch. I have known several folks who got started bird-watching only after they built a feeder and saw how many winged friends came to visit. Some of the nation's most dedicated bird-watchers launched their hobby in this way.

Like bat houses, bird feeders also serve as terrific sources of family fun (and, for many, their occupants are more pleasing to look at). Children and the elderly are delighted by the many bird sightings a feeder provides daily. One friend told me that since he built and installed a few bird feeders in his yard, the "conversation around the family dinner table increased ten-fold! It really provided a focus point for discussion for the entire family—we loved it so much I built a half-dozen more."

Feeders also attract all species of the ever-so-entertaining squirrel. The antics these guys go through to get to the smorgasbord will create laugh-out-loud belly howls. To increase your entertainment, you can provide deterrents to your bird feeders to slow down the daily raids by squirrels, raccoons, and other freeloaders.

Unknown to some, one of the larger mammals attracted to bird feeders for a freebie is the black bear. While they, too, can be fun to watch, take caution—especially if there are children at home. Bears love birdseed and will go to great lengths to include it in their daily diet. In areas where bears are plentiful, extra caution is warranted—more than one bear will put the bird feeder on his things-to-do list!

Bird Feeder

Tools Needed

- Table saw or handsaw
- Compound miter saw or hand miter box
- Jigsaw
- Screw gun
- Random-orbit sander or sandpaper

Materials

- Round object with a diameter of 9½ inches
- Galvanized screws, 1½-inch
- Polyurethane glue
- Latex silicon caulking
- Finish material such as paint or stain

Overall Size: 9½ in. wide, 16 in. high, 11¾ in. deep

Cutting List

	Part	Dimensions	Qty.	Material
A	Base	¾ in. x 8 in. x 11 in.	1	Cedar
B	Side frame	¾ in. x 2½ in. x 11 in.	2	Cedar
C	Rear/front frame	¾ in. x 2½ in. x 8 in.	2	Cedar
D	Bottom support	¾ in. x 5½ in. x 12¼ in.	1	Cedar
E	Back support	¾ in. x 9½ in. x 16 in.	1	Cedar

Note: Measurements reflect the actual thickness of dimension lumber.

Building the Bird Feeder

Cut the parts to size

1. Use either a table saw or handsaw to cut all the parts (A, B, C, D, and E) to the desired lengths and widths, as noted in the cutting list. Note that the widths (2½ inches, 5½ inches, and 9½ inches) are the standard widths of 3-inch, 6-inch, and 10-inch-wide stock lumber; if you purchase standard stock lumber, you will not have to cut any of the boards to width.

2. Miter the ends of the four pieces (B) and (C) at 45-degree angles so you can frame in the bottom and place them on the base (A). To cut the angles, use a compound miter saw or a miter box with a handsaw.

Bird Feeder cont'd

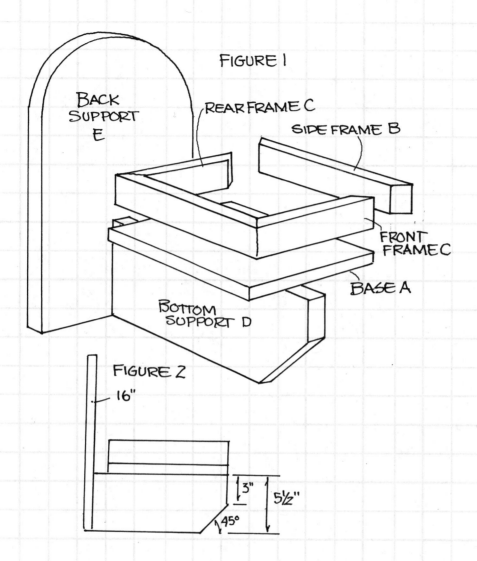

FIGURE 1

BACK SUPPORT E

REAR FRAME C

SIDE FRAME B

FRONT FRAME C

BASE A

BOTTOM SUPPORT D

FIGURE 2

16"

3"

5½"

45°

3. Mark out a semicircular pattern on the top of the back support (E). To make the pattern, you can use any round shape with a diameter of 9½ inches, like a coffee can or plate. Then cut out the shape using a jigsaw.

4. On the bottom support (D), measure down 3 inches from the front and cut a 45-degree angled corner. A table saw or a miter box with a handsaw works great for this job.

Assemble all the parts

1. Attach the two side frames (B) to the base (A) using polyurethane glue and two 1½-inch galvanized screws.

2. Attach the rear and front frames (C) to the base (A) in the same manner.

3. Attach the framed tray (A), (B), and (C) combined to the bottom support (D) using glue and three 1½-inch galvanized screws. Place the tray so that the front is aligned with the front portion of the bottom support (D), and the bottom support (D) is in the middle of the base (A).

4. Attach the back support (E) to the bottom support (D) using glue and two 1½-inch galvanized screws. Make sure the bottom of the bottom support (D) aligns with the bottom edge of the back support (E) and is aligned in the center.

5. Caulk all the interior seams of the tray with latex silicon to seal the edges.

Apply the finishing touches

1. Sand the entire surface using a random-orbit sander or by hand.
2. Paint or stain the exterior surface if desired, but remember that cedar will fare well in the weather if you don't finish it at all.
3. Mount the Bird Feeder in your desired location. You can mount it directly on a tree, the side of a building, or a pole.

Rabbit House

It's easy to keep pet rabbits in cages in a home garage, shed, or outside. Rabbits take fairly well to litter training, so many people let their bunnies run free in the home for at least part of the day, and then put them back in their cages in the evening. Even if your rabbit is thoroughly litter-trained and your house thoroughly rabbit-proofed, a cage will act as a safe haven or nest where the rabbit can retreat to rest, eat, drink, and propagate—as the saying goes—like a rabbit!

Many cages sold for rabbits aren't really ideal rabbit homes, and most are expensive. Commercially made cages are often too small, and many have rough-edged wire floors, which may make cleaning easier but doesn't provide much comfort for your child's pet bunny.

Rabbit lovers fall into different categories: They keep them as pets, their kids belong to a 4-H program, or they raise and sell rabbits for profit or food. No matter why you have them, a spacious kennel helps to keep your bunnies healthy. As usual, bigger is better. If your bunny will spend most of its time in a cage, then build as large a cage as is practical. As a general rule, the cage should be at least four times the size of the rabbit.

There are many different rabbit house and hutch designs. The design seen here is actually considered a hutch, and it's large enough to house a couple of pet rabbits. It can be kept outside, in a garage, or, during the winter months, in your basement—especially if you're raising a litter. (If you plan on raising a litter, build a second hutch of similar design; place them side by side so that you have enough room for a doe and her litter). During very hot conditions, place the cage in the shade and consider placing some frozen water bottles inside it. The rabbits will lie alongside the bottles to keep cool.

This design features a more comfortable wire mesh floor, which makes it relatively easy to keep it clean because the droppings fall to the floor or ground below. The door is large enough so that you can reach inside easily for cleaning, watering, and feeding.

Feeding can be done manually by simply placing hay or other food in a tray on the floor. Or you might want to consider a self-feeding hopper, which is available in farm stores. Simply cut the appropriate shape out of the front or side mesh material and mount the hopper directly to the mesh with clips or wire. We also suggest buying a tube bottle waterer.

This project is both fun and easy to build. If you have kids who want rabbits, get them involved in the building process—it's not only more fun, but also gives the whole family a sense of accomplishment and pride.

Rabbit House

Overall Size:
51³⁄₄ in. long, 36 in.
wide, 46 in. high

Tools Needed

- Circular saw or handsaw
- Hammer
- Tape measure
- T-square or combination square
- Compound miter saw or hand miter box
- Staple gun with ¹⁄₂-inch staples
- Tin shears

Materials

- Common nails, 6d
- Corrugated fasteners, 1-inch
- Galvanized roofing nails, 1¹⁄₄-inch
- Piano hinge
- Hook-and-eye latch
- Wire mesh, 14-gauge, 1-inch x ¹⁄₂-inch
- Self-feeding hopper
- Tube bottle waterer

Cutting List

	Part	Dimensions	Qty.	Material
A	Front corner posts	1¹⁄₂ in. x 2¹⁄₂ in. x 46 in.	2	Cedar
B	Rear corner posts	1¹⁄₂ in. x 2¹⁄₂ in. x 38 in.	2	Cedar
C	Front/rear and top/ bottom plank	³⁄₄ in. x 4¹⁄₂ in. x 48 in.	4	Cedar
D	Side bottom plank	³⁄₄ in. x 4¹⁄₂ in. x 36 in.	2	Cedar
E	Side top plank	³⁄₄ in. x 9¹⁄₂ in. x 36 in.	2	Cedar
F	Long floor support	³⁄₄ in. x 4¹⁄₂ in. x 48 in.	1	Cedar

Rabbit House cont'd

Part		Dimensions	Qty.	Material
G	Short floor support	¾ in. x 4½ in. x 14⅞ in.	2	Cedar
H	Front/rear centers	1½ in. x 2½ in. x 32 in.	2	Cedar
I	Floor corner braces	¾ in. x 4½ in. x 8 in.	4	Cedar
J	Roof	¾ in. x 44 in. x 58½ in.	1	Cedar
K	Doorframe pieces	¾ in. x 2½ in. x 24 in.	4	Cedar

Note: Measurements reflect the actual thickness of dimension lumber.

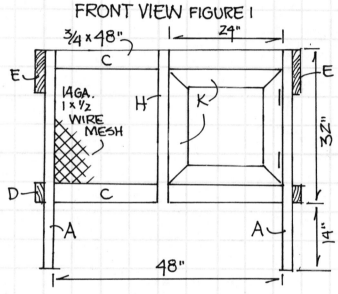

FRONT VIEW FIGURE 1

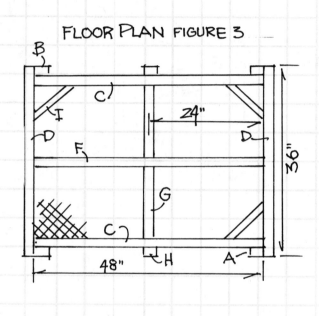

FLOOR PLAN FIGURE 3

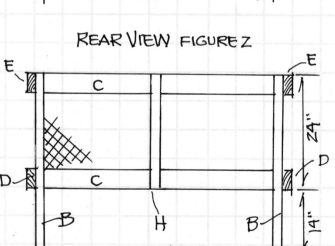

REAR VIEW FIGURE 2

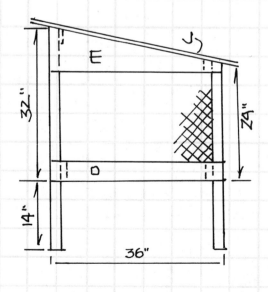

END VIEW FIGURE 4

Building the Rabbit House

Construct the front frame

1. Use a circular saw or handsaw to cut all the parts (A, B, C, D, E, F, G, H, I, J, and K) to the sizes shown in the cutting list.
2. Lay out both front corner posts (A) on a flat surface. Place the two front bottom and top plank pieces (C) in the locations shown in figure 1. Nail the ends together using 6d nails driven into the corner posts. Use a T-square or measure across the diagonal to make sure the assembly is square.
3. Lay out the front center piece (H) on the front face of the top and bottom planks, 24 inches from the right side post. Nail the top and bottom to the planks using 6d nails.
4. Use a miter box and handsaw or compound miter saw to cut each corner of the doorframe pieces (K) at 45-degree angles. Using 1-inch corrugated fasteners, nail the four corners together to make the door frame. Make sure that the four corners are square using the T-square.
5. Use piano hinges to mount the door to the right-hand front corner post.
6. Mount the hook-and-eye latch to the left side of the door and frame.

Construct the rear frame

1. Lay out both rear corner posts (B) on a flat surface. Place the two rear bottom and top plank pieces (C) in the locations as shown. Nail through the ends using 6d nails driven into the corner posts. Using the T-square, make sure all joints are square.
2. Cut the rear center (H) to 24 inches long. Lay out the rear center piece (H) on the rear face of the top and bottom planks, 24 inches from the right side post. Nail the top and bottom to the planks using 6d nails.

Assemble the sides and tie the frames together

1. Position the front and rear frames on the ground in the upright position. Brace them in position or get someone to hold them erect approximately 36 inches apart.

2. Nail the side bottom planks (D) to both the front and rear corner posts using 6d nails.
3. Position one of the side top planks (E) against the top of the front post. Make sure that it is square to the post. Temporarily clamp the other side to the rear post and trace the angle from the front to the rear post. Use a handsaw to cut the angle. Use this piece as a pattern to make the same cut for the other side.
4. Nail both pieces (E) to the front and rear posts using 6d nails. The basic framed structure is now together.
5. Using a miter box and handsaw or compound miter saw, cut each end of the floor corner support pieces (I) at 45-degree angles.
6. For additional support, nail the floor corner support pieces (I) in each of the corners, as shown in figure 3.
7. Position the long floor support (F) between the two side bottom planks and center it on both sides. Use 6d nails to secure it in place.
8. Position the short floor support pieces (G) between the long support pieces (F) and each of the front and back bottom planks. Center the pieces and nail them in place using 6d nails.

Install the roof and mount the mesh

1. Position the plywood piece (J) on top of the framed structure. Place it so it overhangs evenly in the front and rear. Use the roofing nails to nail the plywood in place along the side, front, and rear top plank pieces and the corner posts.
2. Measure the size for each of the screen wire mesh pieces for the front, door, sides, rear, and bottom, and cut them using tin shears. Use the staple gun to secure the mesh in place along the wood surfaces. Make sure that all the staples are securely fastened and hammer any sharp edges flat.
3. Mount the self-feeding hopper and water bottle.

Bat House

Why build a bat house anyway? Well, if you have a lot of these misunderstood mammals flying around your home and property and want to prevent them from making nests in the attic of your home, barn, storage sheds, or pool house, you may want to consider building a bat house for them to nest in. Bat houses prevent unwanted nesting by bats in other buildings. And the bats that live in these houses help to greatly reduce an overabundance of flying, and biting insects.

Throughout most of the United States and much of Canada, bat houses are being occupied by one of North America's many crevice-dwelling bat species. Wherever bats live, they must find enough insects to eat, which largely explains their preference for roosting near aquatic habitats. Bats are a misunderstood mammal. Popularly believed to be aggressive and dangerous to humans, bats are actually gentle, shy animals that rarely wander into the path of a human because of their superb sonar navigation. Bats eat huge quantities of night-flying insects (like mosquitoes) and also propagate vegetation through pollination and dispersing seeds in their droppings.

Building a bat house will provide you and your family many hours to study these wonderful creatures. And you'll get fewer mosquito bites while doing so.

Bat House

Tools Needed

- Table saw or handsaw
- Jigsaw
- Drill with ½-inch bit
- Utility knife
- Screw gun or drill with driver bit
- Random-orbit sander or sandpaper

Materials

- Wood glue
- Galvanized finish nails (2d and 4d) or galvanized screws (1¾-inch)
- Latex silicon caulking

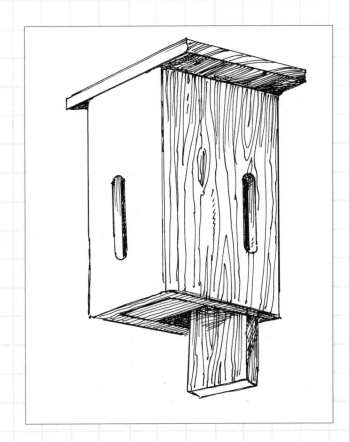

Overall Size: 14 in. wide, 16 in. high, 7½ in. deep

Cutting List

	Part	Dimensions	Qty.	Material
A	Back plate	¾ in. x 7½ in. x 16 in.	1	Cedar
B	Front	¾ in. x 7½ in. x 13 in.	1	Cedar
C	Side	¾ in. x 7½ in. x 13 in.	2	Cedar
D	Roof top	¾ in. x 7½ in. x 14 in.	1	Cedar
E	Baffles	¾ in. x 7½ in. x 10 in.	3	Cedar
F	Floor	¾ in. x 7½ in. x 3½ in.	1	Cedar

Note: Measurements reflect the actual thickness of dimension lumber.

Building the Bat House

Cut and shape the parts

1. Use a handsaw or table saw to cut all the parts (A, B, C, D, E, and F) to the desired length and width. Note that the width (7½ inches) is the standard width of 8-inch-wide stock lumber.

2. Using a jigsaw, cut 3-inch x ½-inch vent holes in the two sides (C) and the front (B). Start the hole by drilling ½-inch holes on 3-inch centers. Start the lower portion of the vent hole approximately 3 inches from the bottom of the sides and front.

3. Using a utility knife, roughen all interior surfaces with horizontal scratches or grooves ¼ inch to ½ inch apart. Do this to the bottom

Bat House cont'd

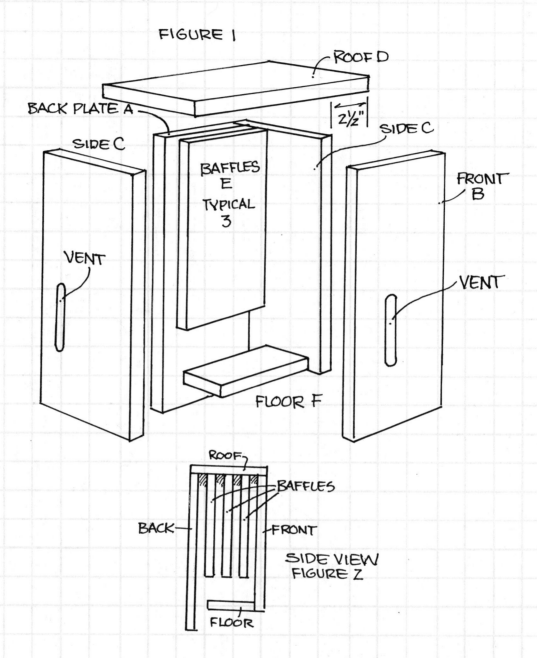

FIGURE I

ROOF D

BACK PLATE A

SIDE C

2½"

SIDE C

BAFFLES E TYPICAL 3

FRONT B

VENT

VENT

FLOOR F

ROOF

BAFFLES

BACK

FRONT

FLOOR

SIDE VIEW FIGURE Z

portion of the landing board as well. The rough surfaces will give the bats a better gripping surface to cling to as they roost.

Assemble all the pieces

1. Prior to putting the pieces together, be sure that the rough side of the cedar faces the inside.
2. Attach the sides (C) to the back plate (A) using wood glue and wood screws or finishing nails. The top ends of the sides should align with the top end of the back plate. The long length on

the bottom serves as a landing board. Predrill all holes to prevent the wood from splitting.

3. Attach the roof (D) to the sides and back plate using wood glue and screws. The extended ends of the roof should overhang evenly on both sides.
4. Caulk all the interior seams with latex silicon to seal the roosting chamber.
5. Position the box so that the back plate rests on a tabletop and the sides and the roof extend upwards.

6. Attach the first baffle (E) using glue and wood screws from the outer sides. Use some ¾-inch scrap material as a spacer to ensure the correct gap between the back piece and the baffle. Working toward the front, repeat this process to attach the remaining two baffles.

7. Secure the front (B) to the sides and top roof (F) using wood glue and wood screws.

8. Attach the floor using glue and wood screws. Screw from the sides and the front, leaving the space opening toward the back plate. Attaching the floor at a slight downward angle will help keep the bottom clean by allowing the feces and urine deposits to fall out the bottom.

Apply the finishing touches

1. Sand the exterior surfaces using a random-orbit sander or by hand.

2. Paint or stain the exterior surface if desired, but remember that cedar fares well even with no finish at all.

3. Mount the bat house in your desired location. You can make a few more houses of similar design, mount them in a group, and face them in different directions. This will provide a range of temperatures for bats to select from.

CHAPTER 8

Permanent Tree Stand Projects

- A Discussion of Tree Stands
- Gotcha Tree Stand
- Buddy Sidekick Tree Stand
- Stump-Sitter Tree Stand
- Master Hunter's Tree Stand

A DISCUSSION OF TREE STANDS

Long before the portable tree stand came on the market, hunters built stands in trees. The stands they erected ranged in style from two simple pieces of strong wood that acted as cross sections high in a tree, to steps made from nearby trees, to flat wooden platforms just wide enough to perch on. The more sophisticated stands had a few heavy-duty 2x4 rafters perched high in a tree, several steps made from cut lumber, and a piece of pine to stand on comfortably, surrounded by a few flimsy safety railings. Although not the safest perches, they served their purpose for hunters from the early 1920s until the late 1970s, when the first portable tree stands were manufactured. From Maine to Wisconsin to Georgia, countless deer were bagged from these wooden perches every year.

When the portable stand first made its appearance on the market, the big hype was that, unlike its permanent wooden cousin, it could give the hunter many more options. It could easily be carried anywhere on the back of the hunter, it could be set up in almost any tree, it was said to be safer and, most importantly, it gave the hunter more flexibility on where he could hunt. If the wind changed or fresh deer sign dictated the stand should be moved, a hunter could do so at a moment's notice. No longer did a hunter have to worry about climbing into the same old wooden stand year in and year out. With the onset of the portable stands, he could climb into virtually any tree that would support his portable stand. Until today, most of those attributes have been valid and still apply—but not always.

Unquestionably, hunters bought into what the portable tree stands offered them, and they soon became the new craze for most tree-stand hunters. Bowhunters, especially, liked the portable stands. For many sportsmen, wooden tree stands quickly became stepchild tree stands. Even today it is difficult to make the case to some hunters that permanently built wooden tree stands are also viable hunting tools.

But to some of the more seasoned old-timers, like me, having the choice to hunt from my portable climbing stand and my more secure and safe permanent wood stand actually gives me more options. Granted, I wouldn't put my portable stand into storage, but I don't rely solely on it either. A wooden stand, well built and maintained correctly, will not only provide twenty-five years or more of effective service, it will also help you bag more deer.

No matter how light and portable a climbing stand is, it still has its drawbacks. It gets caught in brush when you're walking, it makes noise when you climb, it's often uncomfortable over long periods of time and can be more dangerous to use. A portable stand also has to be packed in and out for each hunt and it is susceptible to the lowlifes of our sport—the tree-stand thieves who are too cheap to buy their own stands, so they steal the portable stands other hunters, leave in the woods for only a day or two. Any one of us who has left a portable stand in the woods only to find it missing at sunrise can attest to the overwhelming, gut-wrenching feeling one gets upon discovering that the portable stand is gone. It not only ruins the day's hunt, it ruins your trust in your fellow hunter as well.

That said, I want to reiterate that I'm not against portable tree stands. I own two climbers and more than a dozen metal stands as well. I believe strongly, however, that the wooden, permanent tree stand is still an important hunting tool for today's deer stalker. This is especially true if one owns land or leases hunting grounds. Under this circumstance, a permanent wooden tree stand is a valid and effective alternative to portable climbing stands.

There are several key elements, however, to making your permanent wooden stands more effective and safe. First, the savvy deer hunter understands that building one permanent stand is not enough. In order to work the wind and play the shell game, you must have at least four permanent stands on your property. With a few different stands on your hunting grounds, you don't have to hunt from the same one every day, or even every few days. You can play the shell game by alternating stands every day. By alternating stands, you won't alert the deer—especially mature bucks—to your presence or apply too much pressure to a certain area of the property you're hunting.

Each permanent stand should be placed in a prime spot—a concealed location that takes advantage of a good view and beneficial winds, overlooking travel routes to and from feeding and bedding areas. For the firearm hunter, the stand should be built as far from the trail as possible while still offering clear shooting lanes to observe. The same applies for the bowhunter, but the stand should be built higher and in thicker cover.

It is also crucial to build permanent wooden stands using quality, treated, exterior lumber and fasteners designed to endure the outdoors. By doing so, you not only guarantee that your stand will last for many years, but also that it will be much safer. All permanent tree stands should include strongly built safety rails and wooden seats. Ladders should be built from the same materials, and the steps should be secured with a combination of galvanized nails and screws. For added safety, especially if you—like me—aren't a lightweight, additional wooden supports can be fastened under each step on both sides of the rails. Make sure you test the distance between steps before building the entire ladder. We shorter guys can't get up steps that are 24 inches apart without feeling like monkeys. It is better to add few more steps for comfortable climbing than it is to risk stretching your legs to get from step to step.

Because trees grow each season, they can loosen and dislodge nails and even boards from stands. It is important, therefore, to check each permanent stand during the late summer, ensuring that all connections are secure. Most often, no additional repairs are necessary. But in a hard, icy winter or an especially stormy summer, repairs are sometimes required. I can't emphasize enough that all stands should be checked regularly in order to ensure their safety from season to season.

If the cost of buying stock lumber is prohibitive for you, mixing both natural wood and milled wood is an option—although, for safety and environmental reasons, it is not an option we recommend. If it must be done, however, you can use steps cut from a live cedar tree (if you don't own the property, ask the owner if this is acceptable first). You can also support the steps by using additional cuts of natural wood nailed under each step. Cedar or locust trunks can also be used as rafters and railings. The base, however, should still be made from an exterior 3/4-inch piece of plywood or from heavier exterior lumber such as 2x6s or 2x8s. A solid base provides greater safety and is quieter, as well.

In this book you'll fine four stands of different styles—each geared to slightly different needs. If they are built according to our instructions and maintained each year, each of these stands will provide years of safe and effective use.

To demonstrate the life expectancy of a wood stand, consider this: more than thirty years ago Leo, his identical twin brother Ralph, and I built a wooden stand on Ralph's property in Warwick, New York. Back then we didn't even bother using treated lumber. The stand was made from a combination of tree trunks from nearby cedar trees and store-bought Douglas fir lumber. It was more than 20 feet high and the platform was made of thin, half-inch plywood. I bowhunted from the stand last fall. Not only is the stand still functional, it is also still safe. Every year we check it, and over the last thirty years it has required only minimal upkeep. This story demonstrates how long a well-maintained wooden stand can last—especially if it is made from treated lumber and galvanized screws and nails.

I have taken many mature bucks from permanent tree stands—not only on my farm but in many other places that I have hunted throughout North America. Give the old wooden stand half a chance on your hunting ground and it will prove to be worth its weight in gold. That's a fact you can take to the deer hunting bank.

Gotcha Tree Stand

This tree stand is one of the simpler designs to build. The actual steps to the platform are made by screwing and nailing 2x4s to the two main tree trunks instead of building a separate ladder to attach to the two trees. Once you have decided on the height of the platform (at least 13 to 15 feet high), you should build it on the ground and then install it from the ladder built between the trees. The platform is a comfortable 36-inch-long by 24-inch-wide plywood deck, much larger than most portable climbing stands. This particular style calls for a safety rail installed on one side of the stand. Another rail can be made to provide additional safety and comfort. Consider securing a small, comfortable seat to the platform. A seat allows the hunter to sit facing the predominant travel route of deer in the area. If the travel routes where you build this stand vary a lot, you may want to use a five-gallon bucket (painted camouflage) or a small portable seat instead of a permanently installed one. For additional safety and quietness, I secure the bucket or portable seat to one of the tree trunks with a ratchet strap.

The most important requirement is to select a pair of trees that are at least 16 inches in diameter, healthy, and not separated from each other at the platform height by more than 40 inches. Choosing large trees that are appropriately spaced prevents the stand from rocking back and forth in strong winds. We recommend using treated ACQ lumber because it is stronger and more durable in the weather.

Gotcha Tree Stand

Tools Needed

- Handsaw or circular saw
- Drill and $1/16$-inch drill bit
- Screw gun or drill with driver set
- Air-powered nail gun with 16d nails
- Torpedo level
- Extension ladder
- Safety belt
- Chain saw, hand-pruning saw, or pole saw

Materials

- Hot-dipped galvanized nails, 16d
- Exterior deck screws: $1½$-inch, $2½$-inch, 3-inch
- Nails, 20d, and/or hooks
- Nylon rope, 20 feet
- Spray paint, black, brown, and green

Overall Size: 36 in. long, 24 in. wide, 15 ft. high

Cutting List

	Part	Dimensions	Qty.	Material
A	Tree steps	$1½$ in. x $3½$ in. x 36–50 in.	10–11	Pressure-treated ACQ
B	Long platform supports	$1½$ in. x $5½$ in. x 36 in.	2	Pressure-treated ACQ
C	Short platform supports	$1½$ in. x $5½$ in. x 24 in.	2	Pressure-treated ACQ
D	Platform angle supports	$1½$ in. x $5½$ in. x 48 in.	2	Pressure-treated ACQ
E	Safety railing	$1½$ in. x $3½$ in. x 56 in.	1	Pressure-treated ACQ
F	Platform	$¾$ in. x 26 in. x 36 in.	2	Exterior plywood
G	Seat brace	$1½$ in. x $3½$ in. x 16 in.	1	Pressure-treated ACQ
H	Seat platform	$¾$ in. x 15 in. x 15 in.	1	Exterior plywood
I	Seat support	$1½$ in. x $3½$ in. x 17 in.	1	Pressure-treated ACQ

Note: Measurements reflect the actual thickness of dimension lumber.

Gotcha Tree Stand cont'd

FRONT VIEW

FIGURE 1

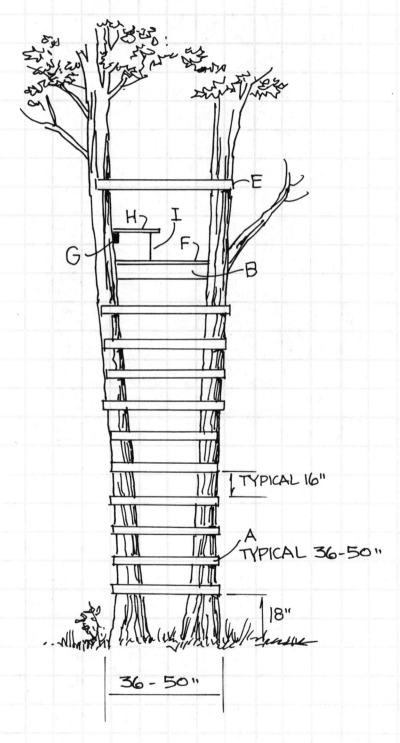

TYPICAL 16"

A
TYPICAL 36-50"

18"

36 - 50"

SIDE VIEW

FIGURE 2

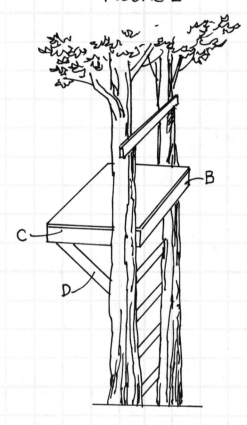

TOP VIEW

FIGURE 3

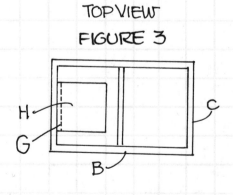

Building the Gotcha Tree Stand

Construct the steps

1. As you build the stand, use a handsaw or circular saw to cut each piece to the required length.

2. Install the first step (A) approximately 18 inches from the ground. Secure it to the tree using one 16d nail into the tree on each side of the step. The nails should be nailed in the middle of the 2x4. If you have access to an air-powered nail gun I highly recommend its use. It will save you lots of time and energy as you are nailing the pieces to the trees.

3. Provide additional support by driving two 3-inch decking screws through each side of the steps and into the tree. Using a drill and $1/16$-inch drill bit, predrill each hole to avoid splitting the 2x4. Use a small torpedo level to make sure that the steps are level.

Working your way from the ground up, level each step as it's nailed in place.

4. Repeat this same procedure for the remaining steps (A) until you have reached the desired height of the platform. For our stand, the height is 15 feet and the steps are spaced 16 inches apart. Depending on the tree width and the angle of the trees, the length of the steps may vary, getting slightly longer as you progress up the tree trunk. Make sure that the steps are at least 3 inches wider than the span of the trees so that the nails and the screws are not at the edges of the steps. You may want to leave the steps even longer, and then trim them to size after they're nailed and screwed in place to minimize the chance of splitting the ends.

5. The first five or six steps can be installed from ground level. As you get higher, we recommend using an extension ladder with a safety belt secured to the tree for additional protection. If a ladder is not available, work from the steps as you progress up the tree. Make sure you use a safety belt.

Use a well-secured extension ladder and safety belt to install the upper steps.

Gotcha Tree Stand cont'd

Build the platform

1. Measure the distance between the inside of the two trees at the location of the platform. For our tree stand, this distance was 37½ inches. The long platform supports (B) should be 1½ inches shorter—in our case, 36 inches.

2. Construct the platform frame on the ground. Lay the two short platform supports (C) on edge approximately 36 inches apart. Secure the short supports (C) to the long supports (B) by nailing a 16d nail through the short support and into the end of the long platform support. Provide additional rigidity by driving two screws on each side of the nail and into the end of the long support. Before driving the screws, predrill each hole to avoid splitting. Repeat this same procedure for the three other corners.

3. Position yourself up the tree either on the tree steps or using an extension ladder. Hoist the platform frame up to the proper height using a rope. Get help from your partner to hold the platform in position as you mount it to the trees. Once the platform is in place, secure the short support into the tree using two 16d nails. Use a small level to ensure that the platform is level. Repeat this for the short support on the other side. Provide additional support by securing the sides to the tree by using at least two 3-inch deck screws driven into the tree on each side.

4. Using a handsaw or circular saw, cut the ends of the braces at 45-degree angles. Install the braces (D) on the bottom of the platform on both sides. Secure them to the bottom using 2½-inch decking screws. Secure the other ends into the tree by using at least two 3-inch decking screws driven into the tree.

5. Cut the plywood platform (F) to size. Cut it so that it overhangs the edges by approximately 1 inch on the front and rear edges.

6. Secure the plywood platform (F) to the platform frame using 1½-inch nails or screws driven into the edges of the platform frame. For additional

Raise the platform using a rope, then level it and nail it in place.

Adding a second section of flooring lends additional stability to the platform.

support and durability, we installed a second plywood platform and secured it in place with 1½-inch wood screws.

Install the safety railing and seat

1. Install the safety railing (E) on the same side as the steps. Place it approximately 36 inches above the bottom of the platform and secure it to both trees using at least two 3-inch wood screws into each tree.

Mount the seat to the tree using 3 in. screws.

Adding an extra railing above the seat is a worthwhile safety precaution.

in the top end of the seat support. Secure the bottom of the seat support to the bottom platform by using a 2½-inch wood screw and toenail it into the platform.

Note: Another option is to assemble the seat on the ground, hoist it up with a rope, and then install it on the platform as described above.

2. Place the seat brace (G) against the side of the tree where you want the seat, approximately 17 inches from the bottom of the platform. Secure it to the tree by driving three 3-inch screws into the tree.
3. Position the seat platform (H) on top of the seat brace (G) and secure it by drilling four 1½-inch decking screws into the brace.
4. Place the seat support (I) in the middle of the front of the seat. Screw the seat bottom to the seat support by screwing two 2½-inch screws

Building the seat on the ground is often easier than trying to build it in place.

Gotcha Tree Stand cont'd

Apply the finishing touches

1. Using several different colors of exterior spray paint (brown, black, and green) paint the tree stand steps, platform, and railing so the whole assembly blends in with the trees.

2. Place several hooks or 20d nails at various heights above the platform. They'll come in handy for hanging your bow, gun, and other accessories.

3. Measure and cut a piece of nylon cord and secure it to the top of the platform. This cord can be used to pull up your bow or gun safely.

4. Using a chain saw, hand-pruning saw or pole saw, trim any overhanging branches or limbs from around the stand.

Buddy Sidekick Tree Stand

This stand was designed to be our largest and most sturdy, which also makes it the heaviest of the four tree stands in this book. The platform is so large and strong that it will accommodate two adults quite comfortably. The Buddy Sidekick Tree Stand allows you to invite either a non-hunting companion with you to experience the excitement of your hunt (a child, wife, or friend) or a beginning hunter who you would like to walk through taking a first deer. In either case, this stand provides enough platform space for two to sit safely and comfortably during the hunt. The platform measures approximately 48 inches x 48 inches, and it is our only stand with two seats.

We attach this stand using a $^3/_8$-inch threaded rod. The rod is about 4 feet long; it fits around at least two tree trunks and is secured with $^3/_8$-inch nuts and washers. The stand must be attached to healthy, tall trees with trunk diameters of at least 18 inches. We prefer to attach this stand to a group of oaks. The stand should be set in a group of trees (at least three or four) or one very large tree with a few good-sized branches growing from it.

This tree stand is one of my favorites because it is designed to provide the most height. The height of the platform on this stand is approximately 15 feet, when using 16-foot side rungs. Since 2x4s are not readily available in longer lengths, making the platform any higher isn't possible unless you extend the side rungs by bolting two pieces together. We don't, however, recommend bolting the 2x4s together because it weakens the stand and makes it heavier and more cumbersome to move.

Although it is definitely intended to be mounted as a permanent stand in a single location, the Buddy Sidekick can be relocated if absolutely necessary—just remove the mounting bolts and rods used to secure it to the tree. Unlike a semiportable stand, however, this stand will require up to three or four strong people to move it.

For this stand, as with all the stands, we strongly recommend building it—including all rails, steps, braces, and supports—from pressure-treated ACQ lumber. If you use pressure-treated lumber, this stand will endure the extra weight of a second adult while still remaining strong and durable over the years. Just be sure to check it at least twice a year, making sure nothing needs to be secured or replaced.

Buddy Sidekick Tree Stand

Tools Needed

- Handsaw or circular saw
- Drill and bit set
- Air-powered nail gun with 16d nails
- Screw gun or drill and driver set
- Hand miter box or circular saw
- Torpedo level
- T-square
- Socket wrench or open-end wrench set
- Chain saw, hand-pruning saw, or pole saw

Materials

- Hot-dipped galvanized nails, 16d, 10d
- Exterior deck screws, 1½-inch, 2½-inch, 3-inch
- Carriage bolts, ⅜-inch x 6-inch with nuts and washers
- Two ⅜-inch threaded rods, 4 feet long with nuts and washers
- Nails, 20d, and/or hooks
- Nylon rope, 20 feet
- Spray paint, brown, black, and green

Overall Size: 48 in. long, 48 in. wide, 15 ft. high

Cutting List

	Part	Dimensions	Qty.	Material
A	Ladder tree steps	1½ in. x 3½ in. x 26 in.	12	Pressure-treated ACQ
B	Ladder side rails	1½ in. x 3½ in. x 16 ft.	2	Pressure-treated ACQ
C	Rear platform support	1½ in. x 5½ in. x 48 in.	1	Pressure-treated ACQ
D	Front platform support	1½ in. x 5½ in. x 30 in.	1	Pressure-treated ACQ
E	Side platform supports	1½ in. x 5½ in. x 34½ in.	2	Pressure-treated ACQ
F	Platform angle supports	1½ in. x 3½ in. x 18 in.	2	Pressure-treated ACQ
G	Platform decking	¾ in. x 48 in. x 48 in.	1	Pressure-treated ACQ plywood
H	Ladder/platform supports	1½ in. x 3½ in. x 60 in.	2	Pressure-treated ACQ
I	Ladder tree supports	1½ in. x 3½ in. x 65 in.	2	Pressure-treated ACQ
J	Safety railing supports	1½ in. x 3½ in. x 42 in.	4	Pressure-treated ACQ
K	Side railing	1½ in. x 3½ in. x 48 in.	2	Pressure-treated ACQ
L	Front railing	1½ in. x 3½ in. x 52 in.	1	Pressure-treated ACQ
M	Seat support	1½ in. x 3½ in. x 48 in.	1	Pressure-treated ACQ
N	Seat platform	¾ in. x 16 in. x 48 in.	1	Exterior plywood
O	Seat brace	1½ in. x 3½ in. x 16 in.	1	Pressure-treated ACQ

Note: Measurements reflect the actual thickness of dimension lumber.

TOP VIEW FIGURE 1

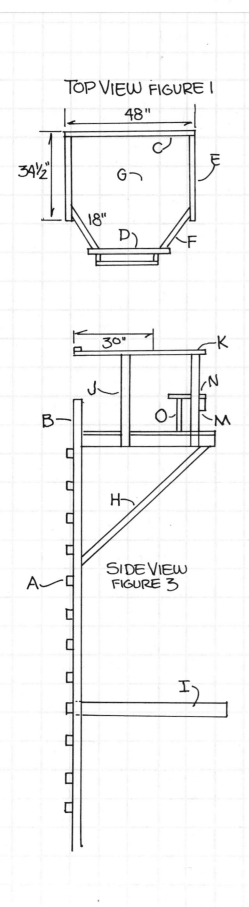

FRONT VIEW FIGURE 2

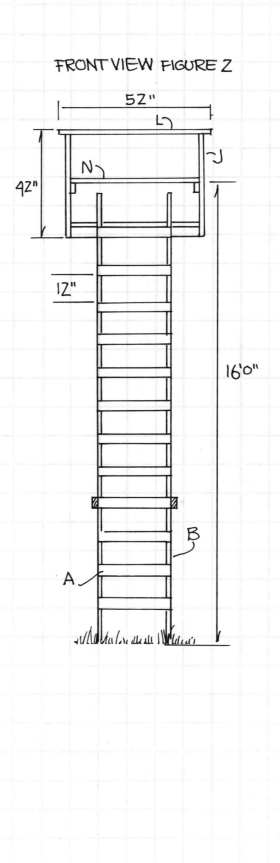

SIDE VIEW
FIGURE 3

Buddy Sidekick Tree Stand cont'd

Building the Buddy Sidekick Tree Stand

Construct the ladder

1. Cut the ladder steps (A) to size, as shown in the cutting list, using a handsaw or circular saw.
2. Lay the two ladder rails (B) on edge on a flat surface. Measure the distance between each step and mark the edges of each side rail. The actual spread of the steps can vary depending on your size and comfort level. For this particular design, the spread between each of twelve steps is approximately 12 inches.
3. Secure each step to the side rails by nailing one 16d nail in the center of the step to the rail on each side. If possible, use an air-powered nail gun—it will save you lots of time and energy.
4. Provide additional support to the steps by driving 3-inch wood screws on each side of each step on both side rails.

Build the platform

1. Cut the remaining pieces (C, D, E, F, G, and H) to size using a handsaw or circular saw.
2. Lay the two side platform supports (E) on edge on a flat surface, approximately 48 inches apart. Place the rear platform support (C) at the ends of the side platform supports. Make sure that the platform support is flush with the ends of the side supports. Secure it in place by driving a 16d nail into the ends of the side platform support. Provide additional support by screwing at least two 3-inch screws into each end.
3. Secure the platform decking (G) to the side and rear platform supports using $1\frac{1}{2}$-inch nails or screws driven into the edges of the platform support frame.
4. Place the front platform support (D) under the front end of the plywood decking, making sure that it is centered. Secure the support to the decking with $1\frac{1}{2}$-inch nails or screws.

5. Cut the ends of the platform angle supports (F) at 45-degree angles using a circular saw or handsaw and miter box.
6. Place the platform angle supports (F) on each side so that they lie against the ends of the side platform support and the front platform support pieces. Secure the supports in place by driving $1\frac{1}{2}$-inch screws into both ends. Also, secure the supports to the decking by using $1\frac{1}{2}$-inch nails or screws.

Attach the ladder to the platform

1. Lay the platform on end on a flat surface. Place the assembled ladder on the front platform support so that the ladder extends past the top of the platform by approximately 14 inches. Temporarily support the other end so that the ladder is perpendicular with the platform. Position the ladder so that it sits evenly between the platform angle supports.
2. Drill two $\frac{3}{8}$-inch holes through the side ladder rail and the front platform support, about $2\frac{1}{2}$ inches apart. Repeat for the other side.
3. Secure the ladder to the platform using two $\frac{3}{8}$-inch x 6-inch carriage bolts, using nuts and washers on each side. Tighten the nuts using a socket or open-end wrench.
4. Double-check to see that the ladder is perpendicular to the platform using a T-square.
5. Cut the ends of the ladder platform supports (H) at 45-degree angles using a handsaw.
6. Place one of the supports against the inside of the rear bottom of the platform with the other end just overlapping the ladder side railing. Secure it in place by using at least three $2\frac{1}{2}$-inch wood screws at each location. Repeat for the other support.
7. Predrill two sets of $\frac{3}{8}$-inch pilot holes on both sides of the rear platform support. The holes should be spaced at least 14 inches apart, starting 4 inches in from each end. These holes will be used for the $\frac{3}{8}$-inch threaded rods that secure the tree stand against your selected tree trunks.

Mount the tree stand, safety railing, and seat

1. Pick out the location and trees where you want to mount the tree stand. For this stand, we look for a grouping of trees with at least two solid trunks side by side because they make it easier to secure the platform.

2. You will need at least three people to erect this stand and secure it against the trees. Have two people pick up the platform from both sides, with the bottom of the ladder on the ground. Position a third person on the opposite side of the tree and have them pull on a piece of rope tied to the rear platform support. Working in this manner, slowly walk the stand up off the ground. A fourth person could be used to brace their feet on the bottom of the ladder to prevent it from slipping while grabbing and pulling up on the steps. If you're using only three people, make sure that the bottom of the ladder is wedged against the bottom of the tree base.

3. Now that the back edge of the platform is against the trees, begin to level the platform by moving the ladder away from the tree trunk. Have one person lean against the front of the ladder, putting pressure on the platform against the top tree trunk. If a rope was used to pull up from the back of the trees, tie it around another tree to temporarily hold the platform in place.

4. Have one person carefully climb the ladder with a couple of 3-inch wood screws and a drill or screw gun. Screw through the back of the rear platform support and into the trees. For additional strength and support, use a 4-foot length of $3/8$-inch threaded rod on each end. Bend the rod to shape around the back of the tree, placing each end into the predrilled holes in the rear platform support. Place washers and nuts in place and tighten the nuts until they're secured to the trees. Using another length of threaded rod, repeat this process for the other side.

5. Secure two of the safety railing supports (J) on one side of the side platform supports. Place the first one on the tree end and the second one at least 30 inches apart. Secure them to the side platform supports using three 3-inch wood screws in each end. Repeat this same procedure for the other side.

6. Place one of the side railings (K) on the top ends of the side railing supports (J). Secure it in place by screwing two 3-inch wood screws into each end. Repeat this step to secure the other side railing to the other side.

7. Position the front railing (L) on the front ends of the two side rails (K). Secure it in place at both ends by screwing two 3-inch screws into the side rails.

8. A variety of seats can be used for this stand design. We have found that a bench seat mounted across the back against the two trees works best and affords the most versatility. Secure the seat support (M) against the trees at a height of 17 inches from the base of the platform. This piece can also be mounted in between the rear side railing supports (J).

9. Place the seat platform (N) on top of the seat support (M). Secure it in place by screwing five 3-inch screws into the seat support.

10. Place the seat brace (O) in the middle front of the seat platform. Secure it to the seat by driving two screws into the seat brace end. Secure the other end of the seat brace into the platform decking by driving 2-inch screws at an angle.

Apply the finishing touches

1. For additional support, secure the ladder tree support (I) approximately 50 inches from the base of the tree stand. One end should be screwed into the side of the ladder side rail and the other end into the tree. Use at least three 3-inch wood screws at each location and repeat this process on the other side of the ladder tree support.

Buddy Sidekick Tree Stand cont'd

2. Using several different colors of exterior spray paint (brown, black, and green) paint the tree stand steps, platform, and railings so the stand blends in with the trees.

3. Use hooks or 20d nails and place several of them at heights above the platform. These make good spots to hang your bow, gun, and other accessories.

4. To safely pull up your gun or bow, cut a piece of nylon cord about 20 feet long and secure it to the top of the platform.

5. Using a chain saw, hand-pruning saw, or pole saw, trim any overhanging branches or limbs from around the tree stand.

Stump-Sitter Tree Stand

This tree stand is one of our favorite designs. Although it can be permanently mounted to a tree, it can easily be relocated by simply removing the mounting bolts used to secure it in place. This design requires you to find a single tree that provides a solid trunk at least 14 to 16 inches in diameter, without any large dead branches hanging above the platform. The tree stand should be placed in a group of trees or in an area that provides additional cover to help conceal it.

Another great advantage to the Stump-Sitter is that the entire construction of the stand can be done off-site in the barn or garage, brought to the desired location in pieces, and then erected. This allows you to build the stand at your leisure. In fact, it also allows you to build a few of them at once. Then you can plan a day to mount one or all of them in the field.

The height of the platform is approximately 12 feet, but it can be made higher simply by using 16-foot side rungs as opposed to the 14-foot rungs we used. The reason we used a lower height was to match the tree line of our particular location—placing it any higher would have limited the view.

Once the stand is constructed, bring it to the desired tree and begin setting it in place. You'll need at least two people to place this stand against the tree and to secure it in place. We built several stands of this design on our farm because it can be built quickly and can be placed in trees of many different types.

Stump-Sitter Tree Stand

Tools Needed

- Circular saw or handsaw
- Drill and 3/8-inch drill bit
- Air-powered gun with 16d nails
- Screw gun or drill and driver set
- Torpedo level
- T-square
- Socket wrench or open-end wrench set
- Chain saw, hand-pruning saw, or pole saw
- Stapler

Materials

- Hot-dipped galvanized nails, 16d, 10d
- Exterior deck screws, 1½-inch, 2½-inch, 3-inch
- Lag bolts, 3/8-inch x 6-inch, with washers
- Exterior spray paint, black, brown, and green
- Hooks and/or 20d nails
- Nylon rope, 20 feet
- Camouflage netting

Overall Size: 30 in. long, 42 in. wide, 12 ft. high

Cutting List

	Part	Dimensions	Qty.	Material
A	Ladder tree steps	1½ in. x 3½ in. x 24 in.	9–10	Pressure-treated ACQ
B	Ladder side rails	1½ in. x 3½ in. x 14 ft.	2	Pressure-treated ACQ
C	Front/rear platform supports	1½ in. x 5½ in. x 27 in.	2	Pressure-treated ACQ
D	Side platform supports	1½ in. x 5½ in. x 42 in.	2	Pressure-treated ACQ
E	Platform angle supports	1½ in. x 3½ in. x 6 ft.	2	Pressure-treated ACQ
F	Platform decking	¾ in. x 30 in. x 42 in.	1	Pressure-treated ACQ plywood
G	Safety railing	1½ in. x 3½ in. x 30 in.	1	Pressure-treated ACQ
H	Seat brace	1½ in. x 3½ in. x 16 in.	1	Pressure-treated ACQ
I	Seat platform	¾ in. x 15 in. x 15 in.	1	Exterior plywood
J	Seat support	1½ in. x 3½ in. x 17 in.	1	Pressure-treated ACQ
K	Platform tree support	1½ in. x 3½ in. x 14 in.	2	Pressure-treated ACQ
L	Ladder brace	1½ in. x 3½ in. x 52 in.	2	Pressure-treated ACQ

Note: Measurements reflect the actual thickness of dimension lumber.

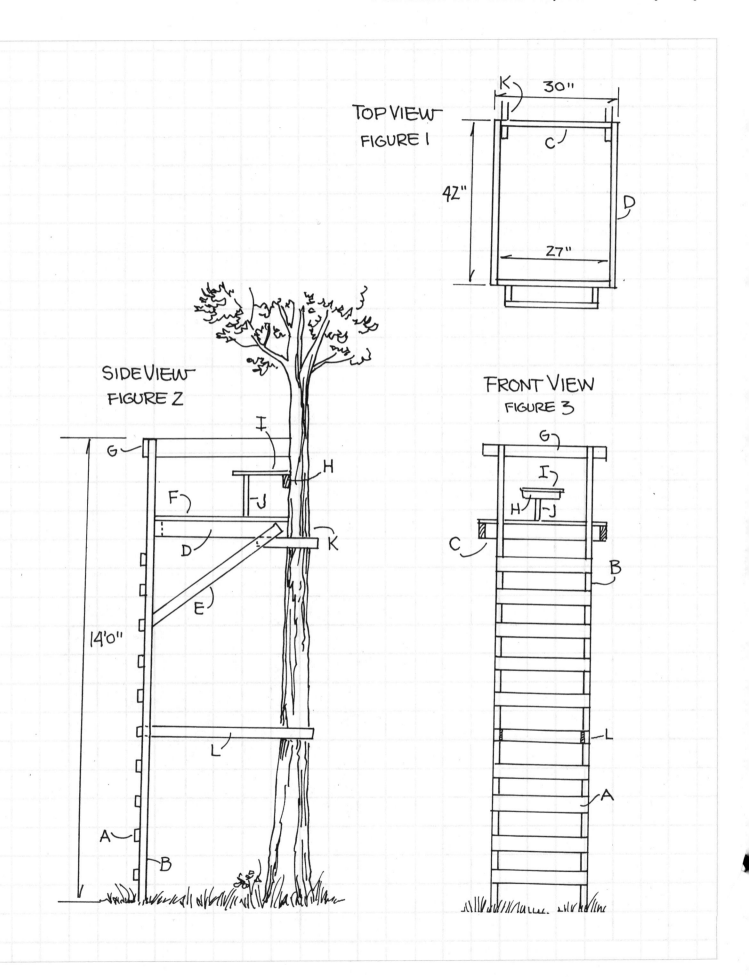

TOP VIEW
FIGURE 1

K   30"

C

42"

27"

D

SIDE VIEW
FIGURE 2

G

I

H

F

J

D

E

K

14'0"

L

A

B

FRONT VIEW
FIGURE 3

G

I

H   J

C

B

L

A

Stump-Sitter Tree Stand cont'd

Building the Stump-Sitter Tree Stand

Construct the ladder

1. Use a circular saw or handsaw to cut the ladder steps (A) to the sizes shown in the cutting list.
2. Lay the two ladder rails (B) on edge on a flat surface, measure the distance between each step, and mark their locations on each edge of both rails. The actual spread of the steps can vary depending on your size and comfort level. For this design there are a total of ten steps with approximately 10 inches to 11 inches between each.
3. Secure each step to the side rails by nailing one 16d nail in the center of the step to the rail on each side. Using an air-powered nail gun will save you lots of time and energy.
4. Provide additional support to the steps by driving two 3-inch wood screws on each side of each step.
5. Secure the safety railing (G) to the top of the side rails in the same manner as described in step 3 above.

Build the platform

1. Cut the remaining pieces to size using a circular saw or handsaw.
2. Lay the two side platform supports (D) on edge on a flat surface approximately 27 inches apart. Place the front and rear platform supports (C) in between the side supports. Make sure that they are flush with the ends of the side supports. Secure at each end using two 16d nails.
3. Secure the plywood platform (F) to the platform frame using 1½-inch nails or screws driven into the platform frame edges.

Attach the ladder to the platform

1. Lay the platform on end on a flat surface. Place the assembled ladder on the front platform support so that the ladder extends approximately 24 inches past the top of the platform. Position the ladder so that it is centered on the front platform board. Temporarily support the other end of the ladder so that it is perpendicular with the platform.

2. Drill two ⅜-inch holes through the side ladder rail and the front platform support, about 2½ inches apart. Repeat this process for the other side.
3. Secure the ladder to the platform using two ⅜-inch x 6-inch carriage bolts with nuts and washers on each side. Tighten the nuts using a socket or open-end wrench.
4. Make sure that the ladder is perpendicular to the platform using a T-square.
5. Cut the ends of the platform angle supports (E) at 45-degree angles using a circular saw or handsaw.
6. Place one of the supports against the inside of the rear bottom of the platform with the other end just overlapping the ladder side railing. Secure the support in place by using at least three 2½-inch wood screws at each location. Repeat this process to secure the other support.
7. Predrill three ⅜-inch holes in the middle of the rear platform support. These holes will be used to secure the tree stand against your selected tree trunk.

Use lag bolts to secure the platform to the trunk of the tree.

Mount the stand and attach the seat

1. You will need at least two people to erect the stand and secure it against whatever tree you

choose. Let the stronger of the two pick up the platform end. With the bottom of the ladder on the ground, start walking the stand up in the air.

2. The other person should brace his or her feet on the bottom of the ladder to prevent it from slipping. As the first person raises the platform end, the second pulls the steps up toward the tree.

3. Now that the rear edge of the platform is against the tree, level off the platform by moving the ladder away from the tree trunk. Have one person lean against the front of the ladder, putting pressure on the platform against the top tree trunk.

4. Have the second person carefully climb the ladder with a couple of 3-inch wood screws and a screw gun or drill. Screw through the back of the rear platform support and into the tree. For additional strength and support, drive three $3/8$-inch x 6-inch lag bolts and washers into the predrilled holes on the rear platform, and tighten them into the tree using a socket or open-ended wrench.

5. For additional safety, secure two platform tree supports (K) to each side of the bottom of the platform angle supports and the tree trunk. Use a screw gun and three 3-inch wood screws in each end of the supports.

6. Position the seat brace (H) against the side of the tree where you want the seat placed—approximately 17 inches from the bottom of the platform. Secure it to the tree by driving three 3-inch screws into the tree.

7. Position the seat platform (I) on top of the seat brace (H) and secure it by drilling four $1^1/2$-inch deck screws into the brace.

8. Place the seat support (J) in the middle of the front of the seat. Attach the seat bottom to the seat support by screwing two $2^1/2$-inch screws into the top end of the seat support. Secure the bottom of the seat support to the bottom platform by driving a $2^1/2$-inch wood screw, angled, through the support and into the platform.

Apply the finishing touches

1. Use several different colors of exterior spray paint (brown, black, and green) to paint the steps, platform, and railings so that the stand blends in with the trees.

2. To hang your bow, gun, and other accessories, place several hooks or 20d nails at various heights above the platform.

3. Measure and cut a piece of nylon cord and secure it to the top of the platform. This cord can be used to safely pull up your bow or gun.

4. For additional concealment, install camouflage netting to the top platform railing. Tie with string or staple the netting to the rails and the tree limbs.

Installing camouflage netting keeps you out of sight to passing game.

5. Secure the ladder braces (L) on each side rail. Hold them in place using 3-inch wood screws driven through the side rails and into the tree trunk.

6. Using a chain saw, hand-pruning saw, or pole saw, trim the overhanging branches or limbs around the stand.

Master Hunter's Tree Stand

With this particular stand, the single most important factor is the location. Because of the design of this stand it can only be built in a spot where three trees are grouped closely together. This design uses a ladder, constructed separately, that can be mounted to any of the three tree trunks. We like to position the ladder in the least visible spot, preferably hidden within the tree line.

You can build the ladder in the comfort of a garage, barn, or basement, and then bring it on-site on with an RTV, ATV, or trailer, saving yourself a lot of building time in the field. The ladder also doubles as a working platform when you build the stand—so you won't need to drag an aluminum ladder into the woods. Before working from the wooden ladder, make sure you secure it to the tree using ratchet straps.

Once you have decided on the height of the platform (at least 13 to 15 feet high), build the platform in place on the trees. The initial securing of the main platform supports to the trees requires a little work, but once they're bolted down, the rest of the construction is pretty quick.

The platform can vary in size and shape, depending on the size and spread of the trees where it's mounted. Try to select three trees that allow you to build a comfortable, triangular platform with at least 34-inch sides. For additional safety and comfort, install rails above the platform on all three sides. A bench seat should also be built on the platform. In fact, the platform is large enough to include two seats so that you can face different directions, depending on the expected travel routes. If you prefer not to erect a permanent seat, substitute a portable seat or camouflage bucket. But remember that a temporary seat is not as secure, safe, or quiet.

One last feature of this stand is the optional roof shed that overhangs to provide protection on rainy days. We also tack up camouflage burlap to provide additional cover from the eyes of deer. The burlap allows us to move around in the stand without being seen as easily.

As with all the permanent tree stands we build, there is no question as to the type of wood to use. Every stand is made from treated ACQ lumber because of its strength and durability in the weather.

Master Hunter's Tree Stand

Tools Needed

- Circular saw or handsaw
- Drill and $\frac{3}{8}$-inch drill bit
- Air-powered nail gun with 16d nails
- Screw gun or drill and driver set
- Ratchet straps
- Torpedo level
- Socket wrench or open-end wrench set
- Chain saw, hand-pruning saw, or pole saw

Materials

- Hot-dipped galvanized nails, 16d, 10d, 8d
- Exterior deck screws, $1\frac{1}{2}$-inch, $2\frac{1}{2}$-inch, 3-inch
- Hooks and/or 20d nails
- Nylon rope, 20 feet
- Carriage bolts, $\frac{3}{8}$-inch x 4-inch with nuts and washers
- Exterior spray paint, brown, black, and green

Overall Size: 34 in. long on three sides, 15 ft. high

Cutting List

	Part	Dimensions	Qty.	Material
A	Ladder steps	$1\frac{1}{2}$ in. x $5\frac{1}{2}$ in. x 26 in.	10–12	Pressure-treated ACQ
B	Ladder side rails	$1\frac{1}{2}$ in. x $3\frac{1}{2}$ in. x 16 ft.	2	Pressure-treated ACQ
C	Platform supports	$1\frac{1}{2}$ in. x $7\frac{1}{2}$ in. x 6–8 ft.	3	Pressure-treated ACQ
D	Platform angle supports	$1\frac{1}{2}$ in. x $5\frac{1}{2}$ in. x 3–4 ft.	3	Pressure-treated ACQ
E	Platform decking	$1\frac{1}{2}$ in. x $7\frac{1}{2}$ in. x 3–4 ft.	6–8	Pressure-treated ACQ
F	Safety railing	$1\frac{1}{2}$ in. x $3\frac{1}{2}$ in. x 5–6 ft	3	Pressure-treated ACQ
G	Top rail	3 in. x 5–6 ft.	3	Pressure-treated ACQ
H	Seat brace	$1\frac{1}{2}$ in. x $3\frac{1}{2}$ in. x 16 in.	1	Pressure-treated ACQ
I	Seat platform	$\frac{3}{4}$ in. x 15 in. x 15 in.	1	Exterior plywood
J	Seat support	$1\frac{1}{2}$ in. x $3\frac{1}{2}$ in. x 17 in.	1	Pressure-treated ACQ
K	Roof supports	$1\frac{1}{2}$ in. x $5\frac{1}{2}$ in. x 4–6 ft.	4	Pressure-treated ACQ
L	Roof plywood	$\frac{3}{4}$ in. x 4–6 ft. x 4–6 ft.	1	Exterior plywood
M	Ladder brace	$1\frac{1}{2}$ in. x $2\frac{1}{2}$ in. x 4–7 ft.		Pressure-treated ACQ

Note: Measurements reflect the actual thickness of dimension lumber.

Master Hunter's Tree Stand cont'd

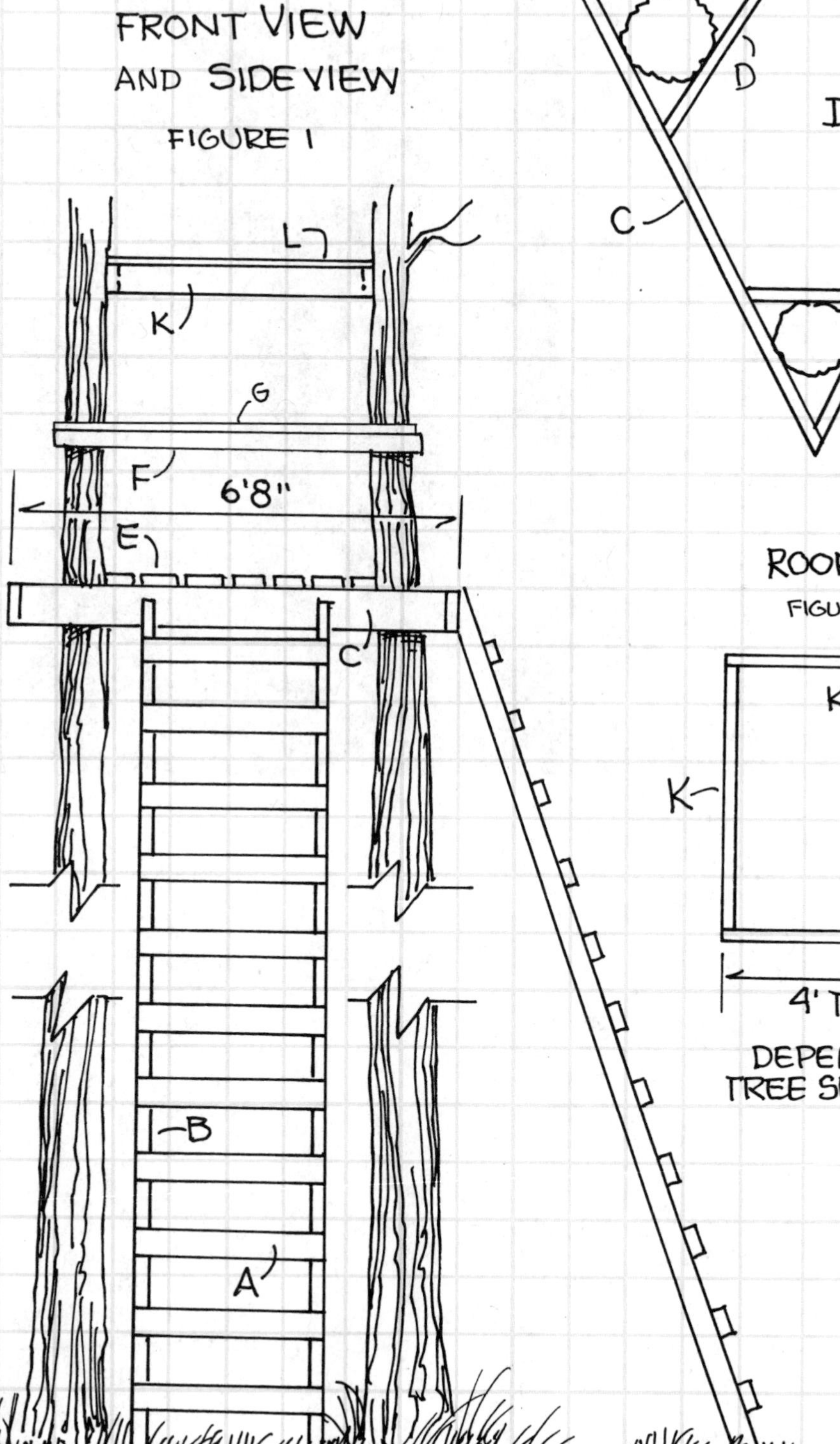

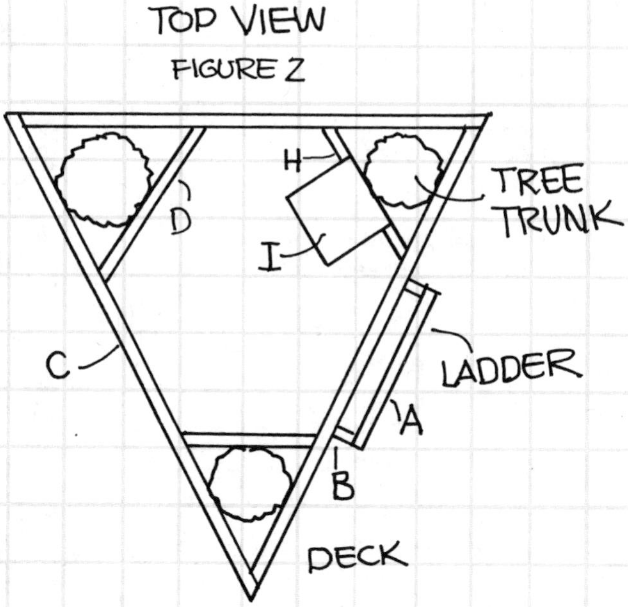

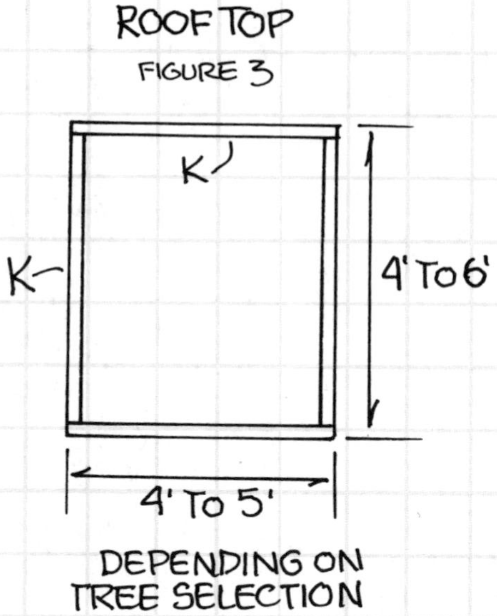

TOP VIEW

FIGURE 2

FRONT VIEW

AND SIDE VIEW

FIGURE 1

TREE
TRUNK

H

D

I

C

LADDER

A

B

DECK

L

K

G

F

6'8"

E

C

ROOF TOP

FIGURE 3

K

K

4' TO 6'

B

A

4' TO 5'

DEPENDING ON
TREE SELECTION

26"

Building the Master Hunter's Tree Stand

Construct the ladder

1. Cut the ladder steps (A) to the sizes shown in the cutting list using a circular saw or handsaw.
2. Lay the two ladder rails (B) on edge on a flat surface. Measure the distance between each step and mark the edges of each side rail. The actual spread of the steps can vary according to your size and comfort level. For this particular design there are eleven 5½-inch wide steps spread approximately 12 inches apart.
3. Attach each step to the side rails by nailing one 16d nail through the step and into the side rail on each side. If possible, use an air-powered nail gun—it will save you both time and effort.
4. Provide additional support to the steps by driving two 3-inch wood screws on each side of each step. Continue adding steps—all but the top step—in this manner.
5. Secure the last step on the opposite side of the ladder. This will be used later when you secure the ladder to the platform.

On a well-secured ladder, begin installing the platform supports on all three sides.

Build the platform

1. Position the ladder on one side of one of the trees. For safety, secure the ladder to the tree with a rope or ratchet straps. Then climb up to the position of your first platform support.
2. Measure the distance between the two trees, add the additional length needed to meet the other platform support, and cut the first platform support to length.
3. Secure one side of the platform support (C) to the tree using two 16d nails. Use a torpedo level to make sure the platform is level. Provide additional support by using at least three 3-inch screws into the tree on each side.
4. Move the ladder to another side, secure it, and repeat the same procedure to install the two platform supports on the other sides. As you measure the supports, cut them long enough so that they meet at triangular corners.

Install the first floor board parallel with the longest of the three sides.

Master Hunter's Tree Stand cont'd

5. Measure the length of the inside angle supports (D) and cut the ends at 45-degree angles using a handsaw or circular saw. Secure them to the inside of the platform support and nail or screw them to the tree. Add the other two braces in the same manner.

Braces screwed to the tree and nailed to the platform supports help secure everything in place.

6. Lay out the platform decking (E), one plank at a time, making sure that the boards overhang the platform supports. Use 10d nails to secure the boards to the supports on the outside edges and on the inside angle supports.

By positioning the floor boards over the braces, you lend additional support.

Nail all the floorboards in place on both the platform supports and the braces.

7. Using a handsaw or circular saw, cut the ends of the platform decking flush with the outside platform frame supports.

Add a rail and secure the ladder

Be sure to nail up a safety railing on all three sides of the platform.

1. Install the safety railing (F) on all three sides, approximately 36 inches high. Secure it to both trees by driving at least two 3-inch wood screws into each tree. Use a top railing (G) for additional support, if desired, using premade hand railing. Secure it to the safety railing by nailing 8d nails into the railing.

2. Secure the ladder on one side of the tree stand. Try to place the ladder on whichever side provides the most natural background. Secure it to the platform at the top by screwing at least two 3-inch screws through the top back step into the side support. For additional safety, drill a 3/8-inch hole through the same pieces and bolt them together using 3/8-inch x 4-inch bolts with nuts and washers.

For additional support, add a brace running from the tree to the midpoint on the ladder.

Construct the roof and seat

1. Place the seat brace (H) against the side of the tree where you want the seat. We suggest approximately 17 inches from the bottom of the platform. Secure it to a tree using three 3-inch screws driven into the tree.

2. Position the seat platform (I) on top of the seat brace (H) and secure it to the brace with four 1½-inch decking screws. Place the seat support (J) in the middle of the front of the seat. Screw the seat bottom to the seat support by driving two 2½-inch screws into the top end of the seat support. Secure the bottom of the seat support to the bottom platform with one 2½-inch wood screw driven into the platform at an angle. Another option is to assemble the seat on the ground, hoist it up with a rope, and then install it on the platform as described above.

Position and secure the ladder on whatever side provides the most natural cover.

3. Provide an additional support midway up the ladder and secure it to the tree and ladder step.

Master Hunter's Tree Stand cont'd

A roof over the stand provides welcome shelter on rainy days.

3. Measure and cut the roof support braces (K) to length. Secure them to the tree approximately 6 feet above the platform using 16d nails. Pitch one side to allow water and snow to run off.
4. Secure the plywood roof (L) to the tops of the roof supports using 8d nails.

Apply the finishing touches

1. Using several different colors of exterior spray paint (brown, black, and green), paint the steps, platform, and railing to blend in with the trees.
2. To hang your bow, gun, and other accessories, place hooks or 20d nails at various heights above the platform.
3. Cut a length of nylon cord and secure it to the top of the platform—it'll come in handy for pulling up your bow or gun.
4. Using a chain saw, hand-pruning saw, or pole saw, cut away any overhanging branches or limbs from around the tree stand.

Closing Thoughts

When Peter and I thought about writing this book, we initially intended to focus only on building tree stands. So we headed up to our farm almost every other weekend and began building a variety of tree stands on our land. Some of these tree stands were similar to what we had built more than twenty years ago on leased hunting property. Others were new designs that we have included in this book. We built more than a dozen different stands that, with annual maintenance, will last for many years. We could easily have focused just on tree stands, but Peter thought by expanding the scope of the projects included, I could share many of my other woodworking projects and skills with a larger audience.

We sat down and drew up a list of projects that we felt would be desirable, useful, and fun to make for any hunting or fishing cabin, lodge, or home. Away I went, working in my shop to build the projects you find here. After almost two years, many of the projects seen in this book have been completed and are being used in all of the above settings.

This book has been an exciting and fun project. The time spent in my workshop provided me with hours of enjoyment and anticipation. Many times I envisioned readers stepping back from a project they built and feeling a sense of pride and satisfaction—those are the thoughts that helped me stay up late at night completing them.

Both Peter and I know you will not only enjoy making these woodworking projects, but will also get a lot of real-world use out of each and every one of them. We hope once you complete several of the projects in the book you will be motivated to start buying more tools and take on even more woodworking jobs—maybe even some of your own ideas as well.

Thanks to all of you for purchasing this book—we hope that you enjoy it so much that we will have to write Volume Two for you! In the meantime, happy woodworking.

Leo Somma

Index

Notes & Rough Sketches

Notes & Rough Sketches

Notes & Rough Sketches

Notes & Rough Sketches

Notes & Rough Sketches

Notes & Rough Sketches

Notes & Rough Sketches

Notes & Rough Sketches